SPOKEN GERMAN

SPOKEN GERMAN
for students and travelers

Renate Hiller

D. C. HEATH AND COMPANY
Lexington, Massachusetts   Toronto

PREFACE

Spoken German for Students and Travelers offers easy but adequate conversational German to students of the language in colleges, high schools, and adult education courses and to travelers in general. The book serves as a basic conversational text for beginners who have no knowledge of German as well as those who already have a foundation in the language. A skeleton grammar is appended for the benefit of those who may wish to consult it. To this end, footnoted references are found throughout the text corresponding to explanatory paragraphs in the Appendix.

For this new edition all dialogs have been completely rewritten in order to make them representative of scenes taken from contemporary life. The dialogs as well as the *Remarks* sections include much factual information and provide some background on German customs and manners, which would interest students as well as visitors planning an extended stay in the country. Some chapters include dialogs and information related to Austria and Switzerland, although most emphasis is placed on the Federal Republic of Germany.

This new edition can also be used as a phrase book, since the dialogs deal with certain common activities or subjects, e.g., playing a game of tennis, getting a car repaired, ordering a meal. Additional vocabulary and useful phrases, following

v

the dialogs, should enable students to express themselves in similar situations. They can also be used by the teacher to formulate questions in German or to prepare additional practice dialogs. Specific points of German usage are brought to the students' attention and are explained in the *Remarks* sections by the use of examples. The index has been expanded to include references to these explanations of usage.

Syntax and vocabulary correspond to current spoken German. With a few exceptions, local dialect and slang have been avoided, and even the sections that have Austria and Switzerland as a locale are written in "Hochdeutsch."

Renate Hiller

CONTENTS

6   Unterhaltung und Sport
Entertainment and Sports

7   Sitten und Bräuche
Customs and Manners

PRONUNCIATION

German pronunciation follows definite rules. Certain sounds and sound combinations are always written the same way, with a few exceptions for words borrowed from foreign languages. The approximate English equivalents of German sounds, where they significantly differ from English pronunciation, are shown below.

I. Vowels

Vowels in German are long when stressed, doubled, or followed by an **h** in the same syllable. They are also usually long when they appear before single consonants. Unstressed vowels are usually short.

a (long)	as in *ah!*	**V**ater, *father;* **Paa**r, *pair;* **l**ahm, *lame*
a (short)	as the first *a* in *articulate* or the *u* in *up*	**A**rbeit, *work;* **a**lles, *all;* **ra**sch, *quick*
e (long)	as in *they*, but without any slide into an *ee* sound, or as the first *a* in *Abraham*	**L**eben, *life;* **re**den, *to talk;* **s**ehr, *very*

e (short)	as in *met*	Mensch, *man;* hell, *bright;* brennen, *to burn*
e (unstr.)	as the first sound in *about*	Lage, *situation;* sagen, *to say;* Auge, *eye*
i (long)	as in *machine*, is usually followed by **h** or **e**	Liebe, *love;* ihn, *him;* Sie, *you*
i (short)	as in *it*	Hitze, *heat;* ist, *is;* Himmel, *heaven*
o (long)	as in *open*, but without any slide into an *oo* sound, or as the final *o* in *tobacco*	Ohr, *ear;* Ofen, *oven;* hohl, *hollow*
o (short)	as in *coral*	Loch, *hole;* doch, *yet;* hoffen, *to hope*
u (long)	as in *moon*	Uhr, *clock;* suchen, *to seek;* nun, *now*
u (short)	as in *bull* or *put*	Mutter, *mother;* und, *and;* Hund, *dog*
ä (long)	as in *share* (in North Germany like German long **e**)	Nähe, *vicinity;* wählen, *to choose;* quälen, *to torture*
ä (short)	as in *bed* (like German short **e**)	Wäsche, *laundry;* hätte, *had;* Kälte, *cold*
ö (long)	as in French *bleu* or *Coeur d'Alene* (Idaho); a close approximation is the *u* in *furl*	Höhe, *height;* schön, *beautiful;* Öl, *oil*
ö (short)	as **ö** long, but short; there is no real English equivalent	Löffel, *spoon;* öffnen, *to open;* können, *to be able to*
ü (long)	as in French *tu* (pronounce English *ee* sound and round your lips)	Tür, *door;* Mühle, *mill;* kühl, *cool*

ü (short)   as **ü** long, but short   Müller, *miller;* Stück, *piece;* Glück, *luck*

II. Diphthongs

au   as in *house*   Haus, *house;* laufen, *to run;* auch, *also*

ei   as in *height*   Bein, *leg;* mein, *mine;* zeigen, *to show*

ai   (rare) same as **ei**   Mai, *May;* Kaiser, *emperor*

eu   as in *oil*   Leute, *people;* heute, *today;* neu, *new*

äu   same as *eu*   käufer, *buyer;* er läuft, *he runs;* Mäuse, *mice*

Note: **ie** is not a diphthong but the German long **i**, which is always pronounced like English *ee*.

III. Consonants

b   at the beginning or in the middle of a word, as in English   Butter, *butter;* aber, *but;* bald, *soon*

at the end of a word or syllable and before **t**, like English *p*   gelb, *yellow*, er gibt, *he gives;* obgleich, *although*

ch   after **a, o, u, au** resembles the Spanish *j:* it is a guttural sound rather like an aspirated *k*   Loch, *hole;* suchen, *to seek;* auch, *also*

ch   after **i, e, ä, ö, ü, äu, eu**, resembles the first sound in *huge* when pronounced with a great deal of friction   ich, *I;* recht, *right;* lächeln, *to smile;* Löcher, *holes*

	in some words of foreign origin sometimes pronounced like *k*	**Ch**arakter, *character;* **Ch**aos, *chaos;* **Ch**olera, *cholera*
	sometimes pronounced like *sh*	**Ch**ef, *chief, boss;* **Ch**ance, *chance;* **Ch**auffeur, *chauffeur*
chs	as in *ox*	se**chs**, *six;* Fu**chs**, *fox;* O**chs**e, *ox*
d	at the beginning or in the middle of a word, as in English	**d**u, *you;* **d**rei, *three;* o**d**er, *or*
	at the end of a word or syllable and before **t**, like English *t*	un**d**, *and;* Ra**d**, *wheel;* Sta**d**t, *town*
g	at the beginning or in the middle of a word, as in English *good*	**G**eld, *money;* **g**ut, *good;* **g**eben, *to give*
	at the end of a word or syllable and before **t** and **st**, like English *k*	Ta**g**, *day;* er le**g**t, *he lays;* Ber**g**, *mountain*
	in the final syllable **-ig**, like German **ich**	Köni**g**, *king;* wen**ig**, *little;* ew**ig**, *eternal*
j	as in *year*	**J**ahr, *year;* **j**a, *yes;* **J**unge, *boy*
k	like English *k*, however it is never silent like English *k* in *kn-*	**Kn**ie, *knee;* **Kn**abe, *boy;* **Kn**oten, *knot*
l	formed farther forward in the mouth than in English	**l**aufen, *to walk;* ka**l**t, *cold;* **L**uft, *air*
ng	always as in English *singer*, never as in *finger*	la**ng**, *long;* si**ng**en, *to sing;* Ri**ng**, *ring*
qu	similar to English *quick*, but pronounced more like *kv*	**Qu**elle, *spring;* **qu**er, *across*

r	produced with one flip of the tongue against the roots of the upper teeth, similar to Spanish *r* (the French uvular *r* is also widely used in Northern Germany)	**r**ot, *red;* **r**iechen, *to smell;* **R**asen, *lawn*
	in unstressed final syllables, sounds like the final *r* in *rather*	Vate**r**, *father;* Kinde**r**, *children;* abe**r**, *but*
s	at the end of a word or syllable or before a consonant it is sharp as in English	Gla**s**, *glass;* wa**s**, *what;* be**s**te, *best;* Ta**ss**e, *cup*
	before a vowel it is soft like English *z*	**s**agen, *to say;* **s**ieben, *seven;* Na**s**e, *nose*
ß	like English *ss*	gro**ß**, *great;* mu**ß**t, *must;* Stra**ß**e, *street*
sch	like English *sh*	**Sch**af, *sheep;* **sch**arf, *sharp;* **sch**on, *already*
sp	at the beginning of a word sounds like *shp*	**sp**rechen, *to speak;* **Sp**iel, *game;* **sp**ät, *late*
	otherwise, same as in English	wi**sp**ern, *to whisper;* Kno**sp**e, *bud*
st	at the beginning of a word sounds like *sht*	**St**ein, *stone;* **st**ehen, *to stand;* **st**ill, *silent*
	otherwise, same as in English	i**st**, *is;* A**st**, *branch;* te**st**en, *to test*
th	like English *t*	**Th**eater, *theater;* Goe**th**e
tz	like English *ts*	Spa**tz**, *sparrow;* Ka**tz**e, *cat;* si**tz**en, *to sit*
v	like English *f*	**v**ier, *four;* **v**on, *from;* **V**ater, *father*

	in most words of foreign origin, as in English	**V**ioline, *violin;* Novem-ber; ner**v**ös, *nervous*
w	like English *v* (Note that the English *w* and *wh* sounds are lacking in German.)	**w**as, *what;* **w**o, *where;* **w**er, *who*
x	like English hard *x* as in *excuse*	A**x**t, *axe;* He**x**e, *witch*
z	like English *ts* in *guts*	**Z**eit, *time;* **z**u, *to;* **z**ahm, *tame*

IV. Accent

1. Most German words are stressed on the first syllable:

   E′rde, la′ngsam, mö′glich

2. The inseparable prefixes, **be-, ent-, er-, ge-, ver-, zer-,** are never stressed:

   bea′chten, entfe′rnen, Entfe′rnung

3. Separable prefixes, like **ab-, an-, aus-, bei-, ein-, nach-, wieder-,** are always stressed:

   ab′fahren, ein′kaufen, nach′gehen

4. In compound words usually the first part is stressed more than the second:

   Schei′nwerfer, Au′tofahrer, Le′bensmittel

5. Words of foreign origin are usually stressed on the last syllable of the stem:

   Universitä′t, Stude′nt, Stude′ntin

V. Capitalization

All nouns are capitalized in German. A great number of

other words when used as nouns must be capitalized. The formal address **Sie** (*you*) and the corresponding possessive **Ihr** (*your*) must always be capitalized. In writing letters all pronouns of direct address are capitalized.

VI. Syllabification

1. A single consonant goes with the following vowel: **lei-se, re-den. Ch, sch, st, sp** are considered single consonants.

2. In combinations of two or more consonants only the last goes to the next syllable: **ver-wun-der-lich, Künst-ler.**

3. Compound words are split into their parts: **Aus-sichts-turm, Ein-ladungs-brief.**

NORDSEE

OSTSEE

Kiel

Rostock

Bremerhaven

Lübeck

Hamburg
Bremen

Elbe

DDR

Oder

Hannover

Braunschweig

Berlin

Potsdam

Magdeburg

Weser

HARZ

Dessau

Essen Dortmund

Leipzig

Düsseldorf Kassel

Aachen

Köln

Weimar

Karl-Marx Stadt

Dresden

Bonn

Rhein

THÜRINGER WALD

Jena

(Chemnitz)

ERZGEBIRGE

Koblenz

TAUNUS

Frankfurt

Mosel

Main

FICHTELGEBIRGE

Trier

Mainz

Bayreuth

BÖHMER WALD

Saar

Worms Heidelberg

Nürnberg

Neckar

Saarbrücken

Karlsruhe

Donau

Isar

Stuttgart

Augsburg

Inn

SCHWARZWALD

SCHWÄBISCHE ALB

Ulm

Freiburg

München

Salzburg

ALPEN

SCHWEIZ

ÖSTERREICH

BUNDESREPUBLIK
DEUTSCHLAND

Maßstab (Scale)

0   50   100   Km.

SPOKEN
GERMAN

1

Allgemeines

Essentials

Alltägliche Ausdrücke

Everyday Expressions

■ **Wichtige Worte** *Important Words*

Ja.
Yes.

Nein.
No.

Bitte.
Please.

Danke.
Thank you.

Vielen Dank.
Thank you very much.

Nein, Danke.
No, thank you.

Verzeihung.
Sorry. I beg your pardon.

■ **Die Begrüßung** *Saying Hello*

Guten Tag.
Good morning. Good afternoon.

Guten Morgen.
Good morning.

Guten Abend.
> *Good evening.*

Hallo.
> *Hello, Hi.*

Grüß Gott = Guten Tag.
> (*used as greeting in Bavaria and Austria*)

■ Das Vorstellen   *Introducing someone*

Darf[1] ich bekannt machen, Herr . . . ?/Darf[1] ich vorstellen, Herr . . . ?
> *May I introduce Mr. . . . ?*

Mein[2] Name ist . . .
> *My name is . . .*

Das ist mein[2] Mann/meine[2] Frau.
> *This is my husband/my wife.*

REMARKS

When you are introduced in German, you simply say **"Guten Tag"** or **"Guten Abend."**

■ Der Abschied   *Saying Good-bye*

Auf Wiedersehen.
> *Good-bye.*

Gute Nacht.
> *Good night.*

Bis bald.
> *See you soon.*

[1] **dürfen,** modal verb, §49.   [2] possessive adjective, §29.

REMARKS

"Tschüss" is a casual form of **"Auf Wiedersehen,"** primarily used in Northern Germany. It comes closer to "See you!" or "So long!"

■ **Sprechen Sie Deutsch?**   *Do you speak German?*

Verstehen Sie mich³?
>*Do you understand me?*

Ich verstehe Sie³ sehr gut.
>*I understand you very well.*

Ich verstehe nicht⁴.
>*I don't understand.*

Bitte sprechen Sie⁵ etwas langsamer⁶.
>*Please speak a little more slowly.*

Ich bin Amerikaner(in)⁷.
>*I am an American.*

Ich spreche ein wenig Deutsch.
>*I speak a little German.*

REMARKS

1. Don't be frustrated by the many German dialects. They are due to the fact that the various regions were settled by different Germanic tribes, who to this day have left an imprint on customs and speech. The common written language is called **Hochdeutsch** (High German). Most people speak it or at least know how to speak it, even if they use their dialect with people from the same region.

2. The Anglo-Saxons also were a Germanic tribe. There-

---

³ personal pronouns, §35.   ⁴ negatives, §39.   ⁵ imperative, §65.   ⁶ comparative of **langsam,** §19.   ⁷ nationalities, §67.

fore, many words in English and German are identical or at least similar. Here are a few: **der Arm, die Hand, der Ball, das Gold, der Finger; die Mutter, der Vater, der Mann, das Haus, das Wasser.**

3.   Other words you will be able to recognize are those that were adopted from another language by both English and German. Some examples are: **die Provinz, das Museum, die Natur, human** (of Latin derivation); **das Chaos, das Drama, der Ozean, die Politik** (Greek); **das Manöver, die Parade, die Armee, der Moment** (French).

4.   Many English words have been incorporated into the German language directly. Some examples are: **der Sport, das Handikap, die Band, der Jazz, die Party, der Computer, das Hobby, das Image, das Make-up, der Teenager, der Trend.**

■   **Nach dem Weg fragen**   *Asking for directions*

Wo ist die Königsstraße?
> *Where is Königsstraße?*

Wie komme ich zum[8] Rathaus?
> *How do I get to City Hall?*

Ist das der Weg zum[8] Bahnhof?
> *Is this the way to the station?*

Zeigen Sie mir[9] das bitte auf[10] der Karte.
> *Please show me that on the map.*

Wie weit ist es?
> *How far is it?*

REMARKS

1.   Note that in Germany, the first floor is called **Erdge-schoß.** Starting with the second floor, the floors are numbered con-

[8] **zum** = **zu dem,** §15.   [9] personal pronoun, §35.   [10] prepositions, §14.

secutively: **erster Stock (erste Etage)** = second floor, **zweiter Stock** = third floor, and so on.

2. Additional vocabulary: **rechts,** right; **links,** left; **geradeaus,** straight ahead; **zurück,** back; **hier,** here; **dort,** there; **bis zu,** as far as; **in dieser Richtung,** in this direction.

- **Häufige Fragen und Antworten** *Frequent questions and answers*

Wo wohnen Sie[11]?
Where do you live?

In New York
In New York.

Woher kommen Sie?
Where are you coming from?

Aus Paris.
From Paris.

Wohin fliegen Sie?
Where are you flying (to)?

Nach München.
To Munich.

Wann geht das Flugzeug?
When does the plane leave?

In einer halben Stunde.
In half an hour.

Wie lange bleiben[12] Sie in Deutschland?
How long will you be staying in Germany?

6 Monate.

6 months.

Wie heißen Sie?
What's your name?

Ich heiße . . .
My name is . . .

Wie spät ist es?
What's the time?

Es ist 2 Uhr.
It is 2 o'clock.

Wie geht es Ihnen?
How are you?

Danke, gut.
Thank you, I am fine.

Wieviel kostet das?
How much does that cost?

Es kostet 10 Mark.
It costs 10 Marks.

Wie viele Koffer haben Sie?
How many suitcases do you have?

Ich habe 3 Koffer.
I have 3 suitcases.

[11] word order, §40c.   [12] present tense for future action, §44a.

Warum fahren Sie nach
   München?
Why are you going to Munich?

Weil ich dort Freunde habe.
Because I have friends there.

Sprechen[13] Sie Deutsch?
Do you speak German?

Ja, ich spreche Deutsch.
Yes, I speak German.

Haben[13] Sie Geld?
Do you have money?

Ja, ich habe Geld.
Yes, I have money.

[13] word order, §40b.

Die Zahlen

The Numbers

■ Grundzahlen   *Cardinal numbers*

0	null	30	dreißig
1	eins	40	vierzig
2	zwei	50	fünfzig
3	drei	60	sechzig
4	vier	70	siebzig
5	fünf	80	achtzig
6	sechs	90	neunzig
7	sieben		
8	acht	100	hundert
9	neun	101	hunderteins
10	zehn		
11	elf	200	zweihundert
12	zwölf	300	dreihundert
13	dreizehn	1.000	tausend
14	vierzehn	1.001	tausendeins
15	fünfzehn		
16	sechzehn	1.100	tausendeinhundert
17	siebzehn	1.101	tausendeinhunderteins
18	achtzehn		
19	neunzehn	2.000	zweitausend
20	zwanzig	3.000	dreitausend
21	einundzwanzig	10.000	zehntausend
22	zweiundzwanzig	20.000	zwanzigtausend

100.000	hunderttausend		3/4	drei Viertel
1.000.000	eine Million		1 1/2	eineinhalb
			2 1/2	zweieinhalb
1/2	ein halb		2 2/3	zweizweidrittel
1/3	ein Drittel		1/100	ein Hundertstel
1/4	ein Viertel			

■ Ordnungszahlen   *Ordinal numbers*

der, die, das   the

1.	erste	1st		15.	fünfzehnte	15th
2.	zweite	2nd		16.	sechzehnte	16th
3.	dritte	3rd		17.	siebzehnte	17th
4.	vierte	4th		18.	achtzehnte	18th
5.	fünfte	5th		19.	neunzehnte	19th
6.	sechste	6th		20.	zwanzigste	20th
7.	siebte	7th		21.	einundzwanzigste	21st
8.	achte	8th		22.	zweiundzwanzigste	22nd
9.	neunte	9th				
10.	zehnte	10th		30.	dreißigste	30th
11.	elfte	11th		40.	vierzigste	40th
12.	zwölfte	12th				
13.	dreizehnte	13th		100.	hundertste	100th
14.	vierzehnte	14th		1.000.	tausendste	1000th

Geld

Money

REMARKS

In Germany banks are open in general from 8:30 A.M. to 12:30 P.M. and from 2 P.M. to 4 P.M. One day a week they are open until 6 P.M. — either Thursdays or Fridays, depending on the area. All banks are closed Saturdays.

Currency: **1 Deutsche Mark (DM) = 100 Pfennige.**
Austrian Currency: **1 Schilling (öS) = 100 Groschen.** About **7 öS = 1 DM** in value.

Swiss Currency: **1 Franken (sFr) = 100 Rappen.** The **sFr** today is worth 10 to 20% more than the **DM.**

Wo kann[14] ich Geld wechseln?
Where can I change money?

Ist eine Bank in der Nähe?
Is there a bank nearby?

Können[14] Sie mir $100 in Mark umtauschen?
Can you change $100 into Marks?

Ich möchte[15] diesen Scheck/Reisescheck einlösen.
I would like to cash this check/traveler's check.

Wie ist der Wechselkurs?
What's the rate of exchange?

---

[14] modal verb, §49.   [15] subjunctive of **mögen,** §52.

Unterschreiben Sie hier, bitte.
Sign here, please.

Gehen Sie zur Kasse, bitte.
Go to the cashier, please.

Zeit, Tage und Daten

Time of Day, Days of the Week, and Dates

- **Die Uhrzeit**   *The time of day*

Wieviel Uhr ist es?
What time is it?

**Es ist zwölf
Uhr (Mittag).**

**Es ist Viertel
nach zwölf.**

**Es ist zwanzig
(Minuten)
nach eins.**

**Es ist fünfund-
zwanzig
(Minuten)
nach zwei.**

Es ist halb vier.

**Es ist fünfund-
zwanzig
(Minuten)
vor fünf.**

Es ist zwanzig (Minuten) vor sechs.   **Es ist Viertel vor sieben.**   **Es ist zehn (Minuten) vor acht.**

Es ist fünf (Minuten) vor neun.   **Es ist zehn Uhr.**   **Es ist fünf (Minuten) nach elf.**

Ein Tag hat 24 Stunden.
Eine Stunde hat 60 Minuten.
Eine Minute hat 60 Sekunden.

Es ist früh/spät.
It's early/late.

Um zehn Uhr.
At ten o'clock.

Meine Uhr geht richtig/vor/nach.
My watch is right/early/late.

REMARKS

1. The twenty-four-hour time system is used for transportation schedules, theater performances, etc. Time is counted

from zero to twenty-four hours (midnight), for example **siebzehn Uhr (17.00 Uhr)** = 5 P.M. One writes **17.30 Uhr** but says **siebzehn Uhr dreißig.**

2. Additional vocabulary: **bald,** soon; **früher,** earlier; **später,** later; **jederzeit,** at any time; **niemals,** never; **jetzt,** now; **rechtzeitig,** on time; **manchmal,** sometimes; **neulich,** recently; **vor kurzem,** a short time ago; **vorher,** earlier; **vorläufig,** temporarily; **stündlich,** every hour; **zur Zeit,** at the moment.

■ **Der Tag**   *The day*

der Morgen morning	**heute abend** tonight
heute morgen this morning	**gestern abend** last night
morgens in the morning	**heute** today
der Mittag noon	**gestern** yesterday
mittags at noon	**vorgestern** the day before yesterday
der Nachmittag afternoon	**morgen** tomorrow
morgen nachmittag tomorrow afternoon	**übermorgen** the day after tomorrow
der Abend evening	**am Tage** during the day
Mitternacht midnight	**täglich** daily
die Nacht night	

Wir sind[16] seit 4 Tagen hier.   *We have been here for 4 days.*

■ **Die Woche**   *The week*

Montag Monday	**am Montag** on Monday
Dienstag Tuesday	**sonntags** on Sundays
Mittwoch Wednesday	**das Wochenende** weekend
Donnerstag Thursday	**jede Woche** every week
Freitag Friday	
Samstag/Sonnabend Saturday	
Sonntag Sunday	

The days of the week and the months of the year are masculine.

[16] present indicative for English present perfect, §44a.

Ich bin vor zwei Wochen angekommen[17].
I arrived 2 weeks ago.

■ **Die Monate**   *The months*

Januar January	**Juli** July
Februar February	**August** August
März March	**September** September
April April	**Oktober** October
Mai May	**November** November
Juni June	**Dezember** December

■ **Die Jahreszeiten**   *The seasons*

der Frühling spring	**der Herbst** autumn, fall
der Sommer summer	**der Winter** winter

■ **Das Jahr**   *The year*

dieses Jahr this year	**das Vierteljahr** a quarter of a year, three months
voriges Jahr last year	
nächstes Jahr next year	**in früheren Jahren** in former years
halbes Jahr half a year, six months	

■ **Das Datum**   *The date*

Welches[18] Datum ist heute?
What's the date today?

---

[17] present perfect for English imperfect, §44c, formed with **sein,** §58d.   [18] interrogatives, §37.

Heute ist der 14. Januar.
Today is January 14.

Das Treffen ist am[19] 20. Mai.
The meeting is on May 20.

Wir bleiben[20] bis zum[19] 3. September.
We'll stay until September 3.

Vielen Dank für Ihr Schreiben vom[19] 1. August.
Many thanks for your letter of August 1.

(im Jahre) 1749 (read: siebzehnhundertneunundvierzig)
in 1749

REMARKS

1. German nouns have several unfamiliar aspects for English-speaking students:

three genders (masculine, feminine, and neuter)
and
four cases both in the singular and plural

2. Articles (**der, die, das**) and adjectives when they are used attributively, i.e., modifying a noun, are declined depending on the gender, number, and case of the noun to which they refer.

Examples are shown in the Grammar Section:
Articles cf. §§1–5.
Nouns cf. §§6–15.
Adjectives cf. §§16–18.

---

[19] **am = an dem, zum = zu dem, vom = von dem,** §15.   [20] present tense for future action, §44a.

Das Wetter und die Temperatur

Weather and Temperature

Wie ist das Wetter?
> *How's the weather?*

Wie wird das Wetter?
> *What's the weather going to be?*

Es ist schön/schlecht/kalt/warm.
> *It's beautiful/bad/cold/warm.*

Es wird regnen.
> *It is going to rain.*

Der Wind hat sich gelegt.
> *The wind has died down.*

Die Straßen sind glatt.
> *The streets are slippery.*

REMARKS

Additional vocabulary: **bewölkt,** cloudy; **der Blitz,** lightning; **der Donner,** thunder; **das Eis,** ice; **es friert,** it's freezing; **das Gewitter,** thunderstorm; **die Hitze,** heat; **das Klima,** climate; **der Luftdruck,** atmospheric pressure; **der Nebel,** fog; **Niederschläge,** precipitation; **der Schnee,** snow; **der Hagel,** hail; **die Sonne,** sun; **der Straßenzustand,** road conditions.

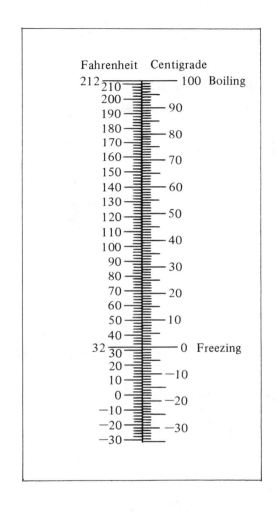

Maße und Gewichte

Weights and Measures

■ **Entfernung**   *Distance*

Kilometer — Miles
1 mile = 1,609 km (Kilometer)
1 km = 0,6 miles

km	← miles / km →	miles
1,6	1	0.6
16,1	10	6.2
32,2	20	12.4
40,2	25	15.3
80,5	50	31.1
160,9	100	62.1
402,3	250	155.3
804,7	500	310.7

■ **Länge und Höhe**   *Length and height*

Zentimeter — Inches
1 inch = 2,54 cm (Zentimeter)
1 cm = 0.39 inches

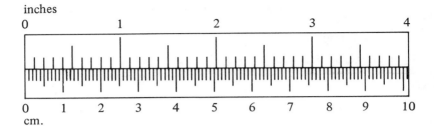

Meter — Feet

1 ft = 0,305 m
1 m = 3.281 ft.

m	← ft / m →	ft		m	← ft / m →	ft
0,3	1	3.3		2,4	8	26.3
0,6	2	6.6		2,7	9	29.5
0,9	3	9.8		3,0	10	32.8
1,2	4	13.1		6,1	20	65.6
1,5	5	16.4		15,2	50	164.0
1,8	6	19.7		30,5	100	328.1
2,1	7	23.0		304,8	1 000	3 280.0

Meter — Yards

1 yd = 0,915 m
1 m = 1.093 yds

m	← yds / m →	yds		m	← yds / m →	yds
0,9	1	1.1		7,3	8	8.8
1,8	2	2.2		8,2	9	9.8
2,7	3	3.3		9,1	10	10.9
3,7	4	4.4		18,3	20	21.9
4,6	5	5.5		45,7	50	54.7
5,5	6	6.6		91,4	100	109.4
6,4	7	7.7		457,2	500	546.8

■ **Flüssigkeitsmaße**   *Liquid measures*

Liter — Gallons

1 gal (US) = 3,78 l
1 l = 0.265 gals

l	← gals / l →	gals		l	← gals / l →	gals
3,8	1	0.3		30,2	8	2.1
7,6	2	0.5		34,0	9	2.4
11,3	3	0.8		37,8	10	2.7
15,1	4	1.1		75,6	20	5.3
18,9	5	1.3		113,4	30	8.0
22,7	6	1.6		151,2	40	10.6
25,5	7	1.8		189,0	50	13.3

■ **Gewicht**   *Weight*

Kilogramm — Pounds

1 lb = 0,454 kg
1 kg = 2.2 lbs

100 Gramm = 3.52 ounces
1 ounce = 28,4 Gramm

kg	← lbs / kg →	lbs		kg	← lbs / kg →	lbs
0,5	1	2.2		3,2	7	15.4
0,9	2	4.4		3,6	8	17.6
1,4	3	6.6		4.1	9	19.8
1,8	4	8.8		4.5	10	22.1
2,3	5	11.0		9.1	20	44.1
2,7	6	13.2		22.7	50	110.2

Schilder und Tafeln

Signs and Public Notices

Achtung Caution, Attention

Aufzug, Fahrstuhl Elevator, Lift

Ausgang Exit

Auskunft Information

Berühren verboten Do not touch

Besetzt Occupied

Betreten verboten No Trespassing

Damen Ladies

Drücken Push

Eingang Entrance

Eintritt frei Admission free

Fahrkarten Tickets

Fernsprecher Telephone

Flughafen Airport

Frei Vacant

Fundbüro Lost Property Office

Gefahr Danger

Geldwechsel Money Exchange

Geschlossen Closed

Grenze Border

Herren Gentlemen

Kasse Cashier

Kein Eingang No Entry

Keine Zimmer frei No Vacancies

Kein Zutritt No Entry

Nichtraucher No Smoking

Notausgang Emergency Exit

Offen Open

Polizei Police

Post Post Office

Privat Private

Reserviert Reserved

Vorsicht Caution

Wartesaal Waiting Room

Ziehen Pull

Zoll Customs

Zutritt verboten No Admission

Einige wichtige Abkürzungen

A Few Important Abbreviations

ADAC	Allgemeiner Deutscher Automobilclub	*German Automobile Association*
AG	Aktiengesellschaft	*Joint Stock Company*
Bhf.	Bahnhof	*Railway Station*
BRD	Bundesrepublik Deutschland	*German Federal Republic*
DB	Deutsche Bundesbahn	*German Railroad*
DDR	Deutsche Demokratische Republik	*German Democratic Republic*
DJH	Deutsches Jugendherbergswerk	*German Youth Hostel Association*
EWG	Europäische Wirtschafts-Gemeinschaft	*E.E.C.*
Frl.	Fräulein	*Miss*
Hbf.	Hauptbahnhof	*Central Station*
Lkw	Lastkraftwagen	*truck*
MEZ	Mitteleuropäische Zeit	*Central European Time*
Min.	Minute	*minute*
MWSt.	Mehrwertsteuer	*sales tax*
ÖAMTC	Österreichischer Automobil-, Motorrad- und Touring-Club	*Austrian Automobile, Motorcycle and Touring Club*
ÖBB	Österreichische Bundesbahn	*Austrian Federal Railroad*

P	Parkplatz	*Parking Lot*
Pkw	Personenkraftwagen	*car*
S-Bahn	Vorortsbahn	*suburban line*
SBB	Schweizerische Bundes-bahn	*Swiss Federal Railroad*
Std.	Stunde	*hour*
Str.	Straße	*street*
TCS	Touring-Club der Schweiz	*Swiss Touring Club*
U-Bahn	Untergrundbahn	*subway*

2

Die öffentlichen
Verkehrsmittel

Public Transportation

Im Flugzeug

On the Airplane

Das ist ein langer Flug von New York nach Frankfurt.
> *That's a long flight from New York to Frankfurt.*

Ja, noch sieben Stunden. Wir sind vor einer halben Stunde abgeflogen[1].
> *Yes, another seven hours. We left (the airport) half an hour ago.*

Fliegen Sie das erste Mal nach Europa?
> *Are you flying to Europe for the first time?*

Ja, ich will Verwandte in Deutschland besuchen und auch ein wenig reisen.
> *Yes, I want to visit relatives in Germany and travel a bit, too.*

Ich bin geschäftlich unterwegs und habe den Atlantik schon oft überquert.
> *I am traveling on business and have crossed the Atlantic many times already.*

Können Sie im[2] Flugzeug schlafen?
> *Are you able to sleep on a plane?*

Ja, ganz ohne Schwierigkeiten.
> *Yes, without difficulties.*

---

[1] **abfliegen,** §§60 and 66.   [2] **im = in dem,** §15.

Ah, hier kommt[3] das Abendessen. Später möchte[3] ich den Film ansehen. Zum Schlafen[4] habe[3] ich gar keine[5] Lust.

Ah, here is dinner. Later I would like to look at the movie. I don't feel like sleeping at all.

Ich habe morgen eine geschäftliche Besprechung in Frankfurt und muß munter sein.

I have a business meeting in Frankfurt tomorrow and will have to be fresh.

Stört es Sie[6], wenn[7] ich nach dem Film das Rollo hochziehe[8]?

Do you mind if I pull up the shade after the movie?

Nein, das stört mich nicht.

No, it doesn't bother me.

Ich möchte zum Fenster hinausschauen und einmal in meinem Leben den Sonnenaufgang sehen.

I want to look out the window and see the sunrise for once in my life.

REMARK

1. Usage:

fliegen, to fly
abfliegen, to leave (by plane); **fortfliegen,** to fly away; **überfliegen** to fly over.

das **Geschäft,** business; store, shop
das **Schuhgschäft,** shoe store; **geschäftlich,** on business; **eine geschäftliche Besprechung,** a business meeting.

Lust haben, to feel like doing something (lit., to have desire).
Ich habe Lust zu lesen. I feel like reading. **Ich habe keine Lust zu lesen.** I don't feel like reading.

2. Close relatives: **der Vater,** father; **die Mutter,** mother; **die Tochter,** daughter; **der Sohn,** son; **der Bruder,**

---

[3] word order, §40a. [4] infinitive used as noun, §2h. [5] negatives, §39b. [6] **Es stört mich.** Impersonal verb, §48b. [7] subord. conjunction, §42c. [8] dependent word order, §41.

brother; **die Schwester,** sister; **der Großvater,** grandfather; **die Großmutter,** grandmother; **der Enkel,** grandson; **die Enkelin,** granddaughter; **der Onkel,** uncle; **die Tante,** aunt; **der Neffe,** nephew; **die Nichte,** niece; **die Cousine (Kusine)** (*fem.*) cousin; **der Cousin (Vetter)** (*masc.*) cousin.

Die Ankunft am Flughafen

Arrival at the Airport

REMARK

Coming from the United States, you will most likely arrive at Frankfurt Airport. Passing through endless tunnels, you find yourself at the passport control.

Americans need no visa to visit Germany.

■ **Paßkontrolle**   *Passport control*

Guten Morgen. Ihren Paß, bitte.
Good morning. Your passport, please.

Guten Morgen. Hier, bitte[9].
Good morning. Here it is.

Wie lange wollen Sie in der Bundesrepublik bleiben?
How long do you want to stay in the Federal Republic?

Ich bleibe drei Monate.
I am staying for three months.

Sie Verbringen Ihre Ferien hier?
You are spending your vacation here?

Ja, ich will auch einen deutschen Sprachkurs mitmachen.
Yes, I also want to participate in a German language course.

[9] For the various uses of **bitte,** cf. p. 38.

1. After the Second World War, Germany was divided into the **Bundesrepublik Deutschland** (Federal Republic of Germany), abbreviated **BRD,** and the **Deutsche Demokratische Republik** (German Democratic Republic), abbreviated **DDR.**

2. Usage:

machen, to make; to do
Du machst einen Fehler. You are making a mistake.
Was machen diese Leute? What are these people doing?
Das macht nichts. It does not matter.
aufmachen, to open; **zumachen,** to shut; **mitmachen,** to participate.

■ **Gepäck und Zoll**   *Luggage and Customs*

REMARKS

Now you have to pick up your luggage. Get yourself a pushcart and make sure you are waiting at the proper conveyor belt. Once in possession of your luggage, you unload it on a customs counter.

Welches[10] Gepäck gehört Ihnen?
Which luggage is yours?

Diese[11] beiden Koffer und diese[11] Tasche.
These two suitcases and this bag.

Haben Sie etwas zu verzollen?
Do you have anything to declare?

Nein, ich habe nur ein paar kleine Geschenke.
No, I've only a few small gifts.

---

[10] interrogative adjective, §37b.   [11] demonstrative adjectives, §32.

Gut. Der Nächste, bitte.
Good. Next one, please.

Usage:
der Zoll, customs; duty
Zoll bezahlen, to pay (customs) duty; **etwas verzollen,** to declare (something to customs).

■ **Vom Flughafen ins Zentrum**   *From the airport to the center of town*

Verzeihung, wie komme ich ins[12] Zentrum von Frankfurt?
I beg your pardon, how do I get to the center of Frankfurt?

Am besten[13], Sie nehmen die Flughafenbahn. Es ist der schnellste[14] und billigste[14] Weg in die Stadt.
It is best to take the airport train. It is the cheapest and fastest way into town.

Wo finde ich die Bahn?
Where do I find the train?

Sie folgen einfach den Zeichen. Der Bahnhof ist direkt unter dem Flughafengebäude.
You simply follow the sign. The station is directly under the airport building.

Kann ich die Fahrkarte im Zug kaufen?
Can I buy the ticket on the train?

Nein, Sie müssen[15] sie vorher kaufen — hier am Schalter der Bundesbahn oder bei einem der Automaten.

---

[12] **ins = in das,** §15.   [13] **gut, besser, am besten,** §§22, 26.   [14] comparison of adjectives, §19.   [15] **müssen,** modal verb, §49.

*No, you have to buy it in advance — here at the ticket window
of the Federal Railroad or at one of the automatic machines.*

Automaten machen mich nervös.
Automatic machines make me nervous.

Keine Angst, die Bedienungsanleitung ist in 8 Sprachen, und
es gibt auch eine Wechselgeldanlage.
*Don't worry, the operating instructions are in 8 languages,
and there is also an automatic money change machine.*

Danke, ich gehe lieber[16] zum Schalter.
Thank you, I rather go to the ticket counter.

REMARKS

1. Usage:
geben, to give
Er gibt ihm das Geld. He is giving the money to him.

es gibt (*impersonal*), there is
Es gibt heute kein Geld. There is no money today.

2. Compound nouns: In German, compound nouns are
very frequent and are written as one word. Compound nouns can
be formed with more than two words, which can be various combinations of nouns, verbs, and adjectives. The gender always follows
that of the last component.

Examples:
die Anlage, installation, machine; **wechseln,** to change; **das
Geld,** money
die Wechselgeldanlage, money change machine

das Geschäft, store; **der Schuh,** shoe
das Schuhgeschäft, shoe store.

---

[16] **gern, lieber, am liebsten,** §28.

U-Bahn, Bus und Straßenbahn

Subway, Bus, and Streetcar

REMARKS

Public means of transportation are quite varied in German cities. Almost all medium-sized towns, such as **Heidelberg** and **Wiesbaden,** still have extensive streetcar systems in addition to buses. In some larger cities, such as **Stuttgart** and **Hanover,** the streetcar lines are being put underground in the center of town. True subway systems exist in **Berlin** and **Hamburg,** while **Munich** and **Frankfurt** have recently built subway lines of more limited extent. In addition, there are rapid electric suburban trains called **S-Bahnen.**

In several cities the same ticket is valid for all means of public transportation: subway, streetcars, and buses.

It is usually cheaper and always more convenient to buy tickets valid for several trips or for a certain period of time (**Zeitkarten).** These are sold at designated outlets or in automatic ticket machines.

Verzeihung, wie heißt die nächste Haltestelle bitte?
Excuse me, what is the next stop called, please?

"Zoo."
"Zoo." (Zoological Garden)

Wie bitte?
I beg your pardon?

Die nächste Haltestelle heißt "Zoo."
The next stop is called "Zoo."

Oh, ich muß aussteigen. Können Sie mir bitte Platz machen?
Ich habe einen schweren Koffer.
Oh, I have to get off. Can you please move over? I have a
heavy suitcase.

Ja, einen Moment, ich mache Ihnen Platz. — Bitte schön.
Yes, one moment, I'll mover over. — Please, go ahead.

Danke schön. Oh, entschuldigen Sie bitte! Jetzt bin ich
Ihnen doch[17] auf die Füße getreten.
Thank you. Oh, excuse me please! Now I did step on your
feet, after all.

Aber bitte, das macht nichts. Darf ich Ihnen mit Ihrem
Koffer helfen?
Oh, that doesn't matter. May I help you with your suitcase?

Ja danke, das ist sehr nett von Ihnen.
Yes, thank you, that's awfully nice of you.

Sie steigen zuerst aus, dann reiche ich Ihnen den Koffer. —
Bitte, hier ist er.
You step off first, then I'll hand you the suitcase. — Here it is.

Vielen Dank.
Thank you very much.

Bitte sehr.
You're welcome.

REMARKS

1. Other useful phrases: **Wo ist die U-Bahn-Station?**
Where is the subway station? **Wann fährt der nächste Bus**

---

[17] **doch,** here used for emphasis.

nach . . . ? When does the next bus leave for . . . ? **Welcher Bus fährt nach . . . ?** Which bus goes to . . . ? **Wann sind wir in . . . ?** When are we going to be in . . . ? **Wo muß ich umsteigen?** Where do I have to change? **Fährt dieser Bus ins Zentrum?** Does this bus go to the center of town? **Die Straßenbahnen fahren alle zehn Minute.** The streetcars run every ten minutes.

2.   Additional vocabulary: **die Endstation,** final stop; **der Fahrer,** driver; **der Fahrschein,** ticket; **die Linie,** route; **die Richtung,** direction; **der Schaffner,** conductor; **der Umsteigefahrschein,** transfer ticket.

3.   Usage: the various uses of **bitte.**

a. Accompanying a request, as in English *please:* **Wie heißt die nächste Station bitte?** What's the next station called, please?

b. Sometimes the German **bitte** stands alone with another thought implied, as in: **Ich mache Ihnen Plaz. Bitte (schön).** I'll move over. Please, go ahead. **Kann ich den Zucker haben?** May I have the sugar? — **Bitte (sehr).** Yes, help yourself.

c. As a short way of expressing that one hasn't understood: **Wie bitte?** I beg your pardon?

d. As an acknowledgment to "thank you": **Vielen Dank.** Thank you very much. — **Bitte sehr.** You're welcome.

e. Sometimes the words **sehr** or **schön** are added to **bitte,** strictly for emphasis.

Das Taxi

The Taxi

REMARKS

Taxis usually do not drive up and down the street to pick up passengers. They can be hired at taxi stands or called by phone. You must pay extra for luggage. A small tip is customary.

Sind Sie frei?
> *Are you free?*

Ja, wohin möchten Sie fahren?
> *Yes, where do you want to go?*

Zum Hauptbahnhof. Mein Zug fährt um 13.52 Uhr. Können Sie das schaffen?
> *To the central station. My train leaves at 1:52 P.M. Can you make it?*

Ja, steigen Sie ein. Wir brauchen nur circa 10 Minuten.
> *Yes, get in. We need only about 10 minutes.*

Ist das Gebäude dort drüben der Bahnhof?
> *Is the building over there the station?*

Ja, das ist der Bahnhof. Sie können hier aussteigen. Das macht sechs Mark fünfzig bitte.
> *Yes, this is the station. You can get off here. Six marks fifty, please.*

Hier sind sieben Mark. Der Rest ist für Sie.
Here are seven marks. The rest is for you.

Danke. Auf Wiedersehen.
Thank. Good-bye.

REMARKS

Usage:

brauchen, to need

Ich brauche ein Taxi. I need a taxi. **Wir brauchen nur eine Stunde bis München.** We need only one hour to Munich. (It takes only one hour to Munich.) **Du brauchst nicht zu kommen.** You need not come.

gebrauchen, to use

der **Gebrauch,** use; **vor Gebrauch schütteln,** shake before using; **ein gebrauchter Wagen,** a used car.

Am Bahnhof

At the Station

REMARKS

1. Almost all of the German railroads are state-owned. The **Deutsche Bundesbahn** (German Federal Railroad), abbreviated **DB,** handles most of the freight and considerable passenger traffic. Its tracks cover about 29,000 km, and all towns of any size can be reached by train. Most major lines are electrified.

2. There are the following types of trains:
Trans-Europa-Express (TEE) — fast trains that connect major European cities. They require a surcharge and have only first class.
Intercity Züge (IC) — express trains that connect 33 major West German cities. They run at hourly intervals during daytime and require a surcharge.
Schnellzüge and **City D-Züge** (**D** and **DC** trains, respectively) — rapid trains that require a surcharge for distances less than 50 km.
Eilzüge (E) — regular trains that make frequent stops.
Personenzüge — local trains that stop at every station.

3. The **Bundesbahn** offers special fares:
Eurailpass — sold to overseas visitors outside Europe, e.g., through US travel agents. Good for unlimited travel in 15 European countries for varying periods.
Eurail Youthpass — sold to anyone under age 26. Otherwise similar to Eurailpass.

Other special reduced fares are available to young people under 26 years for travel only in West Germany. Special group fares exist for people of all ages.

The **Bundesbahn** maintains an office in the US at the following address: German Federal Railroad, 630 Fifth Avenue, Suite 1418, New York, N.Y. 10020.

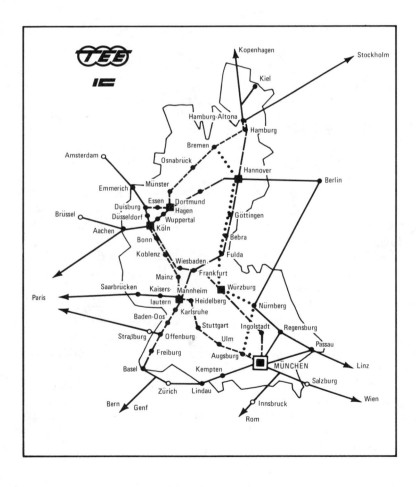

■ **Bei der Auskunft**   *At the information counter*

Ich möchte morgen nachmittag nach München fahren[18].
Welche Züge gibt es?

> *I would like to go to Munich tomorrow. What trains are
> there?*

Einen Moment bitte. Sie können zwischen folgenden Zügen
wählen: Intercity "Präsident" ab Heidelberg 13.39 Uhr,
kommt an in München 17.08 Uhr.

> *One moment, please. You can choose between the following
> trains: Intercity "Präsident" leaves Heidelberg at 1:39
> P.M., arrives in Munich at 5:08 P.M.*

Hat er auch 2. Klasse?

> *Does it have 2nd class, too?*

Nein, nur 1. Klasse.

> *No, 1st class only.*

Was gibt es sonst noch für Züge?

> *What other trains are there?*

Es gibt mehrere Schnellzüge: D 515, ab 14.23, an 18.11 Uhr;
dann der "Rhein-Express" D 215, ab 14.37, an 18.30 Uhr; und
der D 615, ab 16.34, an 21.03 Uhr.

> *There are several express trains: D 515, leaving at 2:23
> P.M., arriving at 6:11 P.M.; then the "Rhein-Express"
> D 215, leaving at 2:37 P.M., arriving at 6:30 P.M.
> and the D 615, leaving at 4:34 P.M., arriving at 9:03
> P.M.*

Danke, das genügt. Später möchte ich nicht fahren. Wo
halten diese Züge?

> *Thank you, that's enough. I don't want to leave later than
> that. Where do these trains stop?*

---

[18] word order, §40d.

Nur in Stuttgart, Ulm und Augsburg.
Only in Stuttgart, Ulm, and Augsburg.

Wie hoch ist der Schnellzug-Zuschlag?
How much is the express train surcharge?

Bis Müchen brauchen Sie keinen Zuschlag zu zahlen. Das ist bei D-Zügen nur unter 50 km nötig.
To Munich you don't need to pay a surcharge. For D-trains that is only necessary for distances under 50 km.

REMARKS

1. Other useful phrases: **Fährt der Zug über Augsburg?** Does the train go via Augsburg? **Muß ich umsteigen?** Do I have to change trains? **Kann ich die Fahrt unterbrechen?** Can I stop over anywhere? **Habe ich Anschluß nach . . . ?** Is there a connection for . . . ? **Hat der Zug einen Speisewagen?** Does the train have a dining car? **Ich möchte einen Platz reservieren.** I would like to reserve a seat. **Kann ich das Gepäck aufgeben?** Can I check the luggage?

2. Usage:

wählen, to choose; to vote (for)

die Wahl, choice; election

In der Bundesrepublik sind alle vier Jahre Wahlen für den Bundestag. In the Federal Republik there are elections for the **Bundestag** (parliament) every four years.

Er hatte keine Wahl. He had no choice.

auswählen, to select, choose

Ich habe dieses Kleid ausgewählt. I have selected this dress.

die Auswahl, choice, selection

Die Auswahl an Zügen ist groß. The choice of trains is large.

nötig = notwendig, necessary

■ **Am Fahrkartenschalter**   *At the ticket counter*

Einmal 2. Klasse nach München bitte.
One 2nd class ticket to Munich, please.

Hin und zurück?
Round trip?

Nein, einfach.
No, one way.

Von welchem Bahnsteig fährt der "Rhein-Express' ab?
What platform does the "Rhein-Express" leave from?

Bahnsteig 7.
Platform 7.

REMARKS

1.   Luggage up to reasonable limits can be taken into the compartment without extra charge. Bulky pieces can be checked through to the destination for a small charge. Most stations have counters (**Gepäckaufbewahrung**) where luggage can be stored for a few days. Coin-operated lockers are also widely found.

2.   Other useful phrases: **Wie lange ist die Karte gültig?** How long is the ticket valid? **Was kostet die Fahrt nach . . . ?** How much is the ticket to . . . ? **Reservieren Sie bitte drei Plätze.** Please reserve three seats.

■ **Word List**

die Abfahrt   departure
das Abteil   compartment
die Ankunft   arrival
der Anschlußzug   connecting train
der Aufenthalt   stop

die Auskunft   information
der Bahnsteig   platform
die Ermäßigung   reduction
die Erfrischungen   refreshments
der Fahrgast   passenger

die Fahrkarte ticket
der Fahrpreis fare, price
der Fensterplatz window seat
das Gepäck luggage
die Gepäckannahme luggage check-in
die Gepäckaufbewahrung luggage storage
das Gepäcknetz luggage rack
der Gepäckträger porter
das Gleis track
die Heizung heating
das Kursbuch railway guide
der Liegewagen sleeping car with convertible beds
die Lokomotive engine

Nichtraucher non-smoker
die Notbremse emergency brake
die Platzkarte seat reservation card
Raucher smoker
der Schaffner conductor
der Schlafwagen sleeping car, Pullman car
das Schließfach locker
der Speisewagen restaurant car
der Wagen, Waggon (railway) carriage, car
der Wartesaal waiting room
der Zug train
der Zuschlag surcharge

Im Zug

On the Train

Verzeihung, ist dieser Platz noch frei?
> *Excuse me, is this seat still free?*

Ja, er ist frei. Der Platz am Fenster ist besetzt. Er gehört der Dame, die[19] im Gang steht.
> *Yes, it is free. The seat at the window is occupied. It belongs to the lady who is standing in the aisle.*

Danke. — Dies ist doch[20] der Zug nach München, nicht wahr?
> *Thank you. — This is the train to Munich, isn't it?*

Ja, es ist der "Rhein-Express."
> *Yes, it is the "Rhein Express."*

Oh, wir fahren schon ab[21].
> *Oh, we are leaving already.*

Hier kommt der Schaffner.
> *Here is the conductor.*

(Der Schaffner) Ist jemand in Heidelberg zugestiegen[22]? Ihre Fahrkarte bitte.
> *(Conductor) has anybody got on the train in Heidelberg? Your ticket, please.*

Hier, bitte.
> *Here it is.*

---

[19] relative pronoun, §38.   [20] here not translatable.   [21] **abfahren,** §45.   [22] **zusteigen,** §45c.

Danke, — Ist das Ihr Koffer im Gang?

Thank you. — Is that your suitcase in the aisle?

Ja, er gehört mir.

Yes, it belongs to me.

Bitte, tun Sie ihn ins Gepäcknetz.

Please put it on the luggage rack.

REMARKS

1. Other useful phrases: **Das ist mein Platz.** This is my seat. **Wie viele Stationen sind es noch bis . . . ?** How many stations are there before we get to . . . ? **Darf ich das Fenster öffnen / schließen?** May I open / close the window? **Wie lange haben wir Aufenthalt?** How long do we stop here?

2. Usage:

tun, to do; to put

sein Bestes tun, to do ones best; **Ich habe viel zu tun.** I have a lot to do.

Ich tue den Brief in den Umschlag. I put the letter in the envelope.

3

Mit dem Auto
unterwegs

Traveling by Car

Der Mietwagen

Car Rental

REMARKS

Avis and *Hertz* have offices in most German cities. *InterRent.* a subsidiary of "Volkswagen," as well as several other companies also rent cars.

Guten Tag. Ich möchte einen Wagen mieten.
Hello. I would like to rent a car.

Ja, bitte, hier ist unsere Preisliste für Pkw. Im Augenblick sind alle Wagen verfügbar, bis auf die beiden kleinsten[1].
Yes, here is our price list for passenger cars. At the moment, all cars are available, except for the two smallest ones.

Ich nehme den Audi 80. Sind die gefahrenen Kilometer im Preis enthalten?
I'll take the Audi 80. Is the mileage included in the price?

Ja, natürlich, aber das Benzin müssen Sie selbst bezahlen. — Für wie lange möchten Sie den Wagen?
Yes, of course, but you have to pay for the gasoline yourself. — For how long would you like the car?

Für zwei Wochen.
For two weeks.

Kann ich Ihren Führerschein haben und eine Kreditkarte?
Can I have your drivers license and a credit card?

[1] comparison of adjectives, §19.

Ja, ich habe eine American Express Karte.

Yes, I have an American Express card.

Ja, das genügt. Hier ist Ihr Vertrag und der Schlüssel. Der Wagen hat die Nummer HD P-122 und steht in der zweiten Reihe von vorn.

Yes, that is fine. Here is your contract and the key. The car has the license number HD P-122 and is parked in the second row from the front.

Könnte mir jemand zeigen, wie man[2] die Schaltung, die Scheinwerfer, die Richtungsanweiser und die Heizung bedient.

Could someone show me how one operates the gear shift, the headlights, the blinker, and the heating.

Ja, natürlich. Ich werde es Ihnen selbst zeigen. Ich gebe Ihnen auch noch[3] eine Bedienungsanweisung und eine Straßenkarte für Süddeutschland.

Yes, of course. I will show you myself. I'll also give you an operating instruction booklet and a road map of Southern Germany.

REMARKS

1. German license numbers start with one or more letters showing the city where the car is registered. Thus **M = München, HD = Heidelberg.**

2. Vocabulary: **der Pkw (Personenkraftwagen), der Wagen, das Auto(mobil)** = car, automobile; **das Benzin** = gasoline (*Benzene* in English is **Benzol** in German.)

3. Usage: The indefinite pronoun **man** is often translated with *one, you, people,* or *they,* depending on the context. Frequently **man** replaces the English passive:

[2] §51a.   [3] **noch,** *still,* here not translatable.

Man tut das nicht. One doesn't do that.
You don't do that.
That is not done.
People don't do that.

Man hat der Frau das Geld gestohlen. The lady's money was stolen.

Auf deutschen Straßen

On German Roads

REMARKS

For an American, driving in Germany can be at first a startling experience. Speed limits exist in cities (50 km/h or 30 mph) and on rural highways (100 km/h or 60 mph) but are widely disregarded. On the **Autobahn** speed is limited only by the power of the car and it is not unusual to be passed by a Porsche going 200 km/h (125 mph). Driving is also made more difficult by elaborate rules of the road and by a multitude of traffic signs.

■ **Auf der Autobahn**   *On the Autobahn*

Wie viele Kilometer sind es noch bis Hamburg?
> *How many more kilometers are there still to Hamburg?*

Etwa 100, noch eine knappe Stunde, wenn[4] der Verkehr so bleibt.
> *About 100, not quite another hour if the traffic stays as it is.*

Wie schnell fahren wir?
> *How fast are we going?*

Zwischen 130 und 140 km (pro Stunde).
> *Between 130 and 140 km (per hour).*

Haben wir eine Straßenkarte von dieser Gegend?
> *Do we have a road map of this area?*

[4] subordinating conjunctions, §§41, 42b.

Ja, im Handschuhfach. Was willst Du nachsehen?
Yes, in the glove compartment. What do you want to look up?

Nichts Besonderes[2]. — Was will dieser Typ, der uns beinahe hinten in den Wagen fährt und mit den Scheinwerfen blinkt?
Nothing special. — What does this fellow want who is almost running into our car and signaling with his headlights?

Er wird es wohl sehr eilig haben[6] und will[7], daß wir ihm Platz machen.
He must be in a hurry and wants us to move over.

Schau auf die Benzinuhr; der Tank ist fast leer.
Have a look at the gas gauge; the gas tank is almost empty.

Gut, daß Du das gesehen hast. Hier ist gerade eine Tankstelle.
Good that you noticed it. There just happens to be a gas station.

Ich hoffe, die Toiletten sind sauber.
I hope the rest rooms are clean.

REMARKS

1. Some rules for driving in Germany:
Man sollte[8] die Verkehrsregeln und Verkehrszeichen genau kennen. You should know the traffic rules and traffic signs well.

> **. . . bei Zebra-Streifen besonders gut aufpassen. (Die Fußgänger haben Vorrang.)** . . . watch out for zebra-stripe crosswalks. (Pedestrians have the right of way.)
>
> **. . . besonders auf Fahrradfahrer achten.** . . . . especially watch out for cyclists.
>
> **. . . auf der Autobahn niemals rechts überholen.** never pass on the right on the Autobahn.

---

[5] §18.   [6] probability, §44c.   [7] **wollen,** modal verb, §49.   [8] **sollen,** subjunctive, §63.

... **beim Parken die Stoßstange des anderen Autos niemals berühren.** ... never touch the bumper of the other car while parking.

2. Usage:

knapp, scarce, insufficient; small
Das Geld ist knapp. Money is scarce. **eine knappe Stunde,** scarcely an hour.
eine knappe Mehrheit, a small majority.

Platz machen, to make room, to move over.

■ **Word List**

die Ampel (traffic)light
der Anhänger trailer
die Ausfahrt exit; driveway
der Bahnübergang railroad crossing
die Baustelle road construction (site)
die Brücke bridge
das Fahrrad bicycle
das Fahrzeug vehicle
der Führerschein drivers license
die Geschwindigkeitsbegrenzung speed limit
das Halteverbot no stopping
die Höchstgeschwindigkeit maximum speed
der Kombi(wagen) station wagon
die Kreuzung intersection
die Kurve curve
der Lastwagen truck
das Lieferauto delivery van

das Moped small motor bike
das Motorrad motor cycle
der Motorroller motor scooter
der Parkplatz parking lot
die Parkuhr parking meter
das Parkverbot no parking
der Radfahrweg bicycle trail
die Steigung gradient
der Tunnel tunnel
das Überholverbot no passing
die Umleitung detour
der Verkehr traffic
das Verkehrsschild road sign
die Vorfahrt right of way
der Wegweiser signpost
der Wohnwagen camping trailer

REMARKS

Streets and Roads : **die Straße** road, highway; street; **die Allee,** avenue, boulevard (often bordered by trees); **die Gasse,** alley; **der Weg,** trail; **die Bundesstraße,** federal highway; **die Landstraße,** country road, **die Nebenstraße,** secondary road; **die Einbahnstraße,** one-way street; **die Haupstraße,** main road, main street; **die Querstraße,** crossroad.

An der Tankstelle

At the Gas Station

REMARKS

There are gas stations with attendants, but self-service stations, which charge slightly lower prices, are becoming more popular.

Volltanken[9], bitte! Super!
Fill her up, please! Premium!

Geben Sie mir den Tankschlüssel bitte.
Give me the key for the gas tank, please.

Hier, bitte.
Here it is.

Genau 50 Liter.
Exactly 50 Liters.

Prüfen Sie bitte auch das Öl und das Wasser.
Please check the oil and water.

Alles in Ordnung. Sie bezahlen an der Kasse bitte.
Everything O.K. Pay the cashier, please.

---

[9] infinitive used as imperative.

REMARKS

Additional vocabulary: **der Ölstand,** oil level; **der Ölwechsel,** oil change; **die Reifen,** tires; **den Reifendruck prüfen,** to check the tire pressure; **die Windschutzscheibe säubern,** to clean the windshield.

Ein Unfall

An Accident

Na, hören Sie mal! Ich hatte Vorfahrt!
> *What do you think you were doing?* (*Lit., Listen, you!*)
> *I had the right of way!*

Nein, Sie sind schuld! Sie sind viel zu schnell gefahren — deshalb[10] haben Sie mich gerammt!
> *No, it is your fault! You went much too fast — that's why you hit me!*

Ich bin schließlich von rechts gekommen! Sie hätten halten müssen[11]!
> *After all, I came from the right! You should have stopped!*

(Zu einem Passanten) Können Sie bitte die Polizei rufen?
> (*To a passer-by*) *Can you please call the police?*

(Ein Polizist) Ihren Führerschein und die Wagenpapiere bitte. — Ist jemand verletzt?
> (*A policeman*) *Your drivers license and the car papers, please. — Is anyone hurt?*

Nein, niemand. Ich bin von rechts gekommen! Ich hatte Vorfahrt!
> *No, nobody. I came from the right. I had the right of way.*

Das werden wir sehen. Ihre Bremsspur ist sehr lang. Sie sind auf jeden Fall zu schnell gefahren.

---

[10] coordinating conjunction, §42a.   [11] double infinitive, §49d, and subjunctive, §52.

We will see. Your tire marks are very long. You definitely went too fast.

(Der Passant) Ich war Zeuge des Unfalls. Ich habe gesehen, daß dieser Mann wie ein Verrückter gefahren ist.

(The passer-by) I witnessed the accident. I saw that this man drove like a maniac.

(Der Polizist) Geben Sie mir Ihren Namen und Ihre Adresse bitte.

(Policeman) Give me your name and address, please.

(2. Polizist) Ich habe den Unfall aufgenommen. Machen Sie bitte die Straße frei.

(2nd policeman) I've recorded the accident. Please clear the street

(1. Polizist) Benachrichtigen Sie beide Ihre Versicherungen. Sie können jetzt Ihre Wagen in die Werkstatt fahren.

(1st policeman) Inform your insurance companies. You can now drive your cars to the repair shop.

REMARKS

1. Additional vocabulary: **abschleppen,** to tow; **der Abschleppdienst,** towing service; **das Abschleppseil,** tow rope; **der Aufprall,** impact; **der Krankenwagen, die Ambulanz,** ambulance; **der Schaden,** damage; **die Panne,** breakdown; **die Verletzung,** injury; **der Zeuge,** witness; **der Zusammenstoß,** collision.

2. Usage: **Sie sind schuld./Sie haben schuld.** You are at fault. **Es ist Ihre Schuld.** It is your fault.

DAS AUTOMOBIL

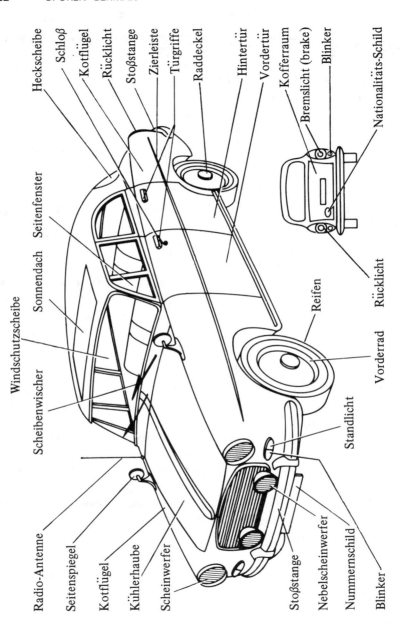

Heckscheibe
Schloß
Kotflügel
Rücklicht
Stoßstange
Zierleiste
Türgriffe
Raddeckel
Hintertür
Vordertür
Kofferraum
Bremslicht (brake)
Blinker
Nationalitäts-Schild

Seitenfenster
Sonnendach
Windschutzscheibe
Scheibenwischer
Seitenspiegel

Rücklicht
Reifen
Vorderrad

Standlicht

Radio-Antenne
Seitenspiegel
Kotflügel
Kühlerhaube
Scheinwerfer
Stoßstange
Nebelscheinwerfer
Nummernschild
Blinker

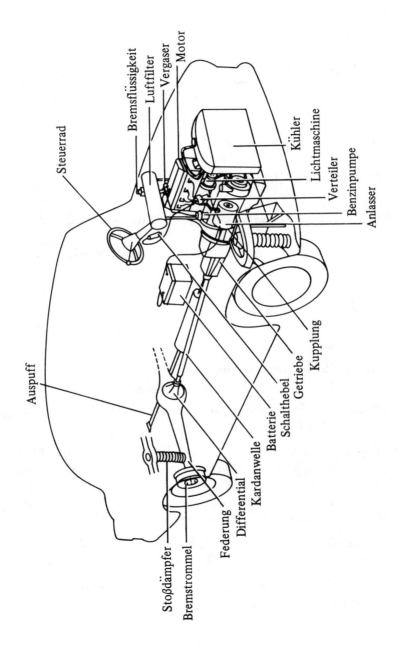

Bremsflüssigkeit
Luftfilter
Vergaser
Motor
Steuerrad
Kühler
Lichtmaschine
Verteiler
Benzinpumpe
Anlasser
Auspuff
Kupplung
Getriebe
Schalthebel
Batterie
Kardanwelle
Differential
Federung
Stoßdämpfer
Bremstrommel

■ In der Werkstatt   *At the repair shop*

Guten Tag. Mein Wagen steht draußen. Ich hatte einen Unfall. Können Sie sich den Schaden ansehen[12]?
> *Good morning. My car is outside. I had an accident. Can you take a look at the damage?*

Ja, ich komme mit Ihnen.
> *Yes, I'll come with you.*

Sieht ziemlich schlimm aus, nicht?
> *Looks pretty bad, doesn't it?*

Ganz schöner Schaden. — Haben Sie den Unfall der Polizei gemeldet?
> *Quite some damage. — Did you report the accident to the police?*

Ja, die Polizei ist gekommen. — Der andere Fahrer war schuld. Er ist zu schnell gefahren.
> *Yes, the police came. — The other driver was at fault. He went too fast.*

Geben Sie mir Ihre Schlüssel und die Wagenpapiere bitte.
> *Give me your keys and the car papers, please.*

Wie lange wird die Reparatur dauern?
> *How long will it take to repair the car?*

Erst muß der Sachverständige der Versicherung den Schaden sehen; danach[13] etwa 10 Tage, wenn alle Ersatzteile auf Lager sind.
> *First the insurance expert has to look at the damage; after that about 10 days if all the spare parts are in stock.*

Wenn Sie schon[14] dabei sind, können Sie auch die Bremsen, den Verteiler und die Zündkerzen nachsehen.

[12] reflexive verbs, §47b.   [13] pronominal compounds, §36.   [14] **schon,** *already,* here not translatable.

While you are at it, you may also look at the brakes, the distributor, and the spark plugs.

Soll ich auch die Batterie prüfen?
Shall I check the battery, too?

Ja, bitte, sie ist schon ziemlich alt.
Yes, please, it's already pretty old.

Übrigens haben Sie nicht mehr viel Profil auf den vorderen Reifen.
By the way, you don't have much rubber left (lit., you have not much more profile left) on your front tires.

Ja, aber jetzt kann ich mir keine neuen leisten. — Rufen Sie mich an, wenn der Wagen fertig ist.
Yes, but now I can't afford new ones. — Call me when the car is ready.

REMARKS

1. Some useful verbs: **entfernen,** to remove; **einstellen,** to adjust; **erneuern/auswechseln/ersetzen,** to replace; **(Batterien) laden,** to charge (batteries); **montieren,** to mount; **(Schrauben) nachziehen,** to tighten (screws); **polieren,** to polish; **reinigen,** to clean.

2. Usage:
sehen, to see; **ansehen,** to look at; **nachsehen,** to check
sich etwas ansehen, to take a look at something

das **Profil,** profile (face); rubber on a tire

leisten, to accomplish, perform
sich etwas leisten, to afford something
die **Leistung,** performance, achievement

4

Unterkunft und Verpflegung

Food and Lodging

Bei der "Tourist-Information"

At the "Tourist Information"

REMARKS

1. The *Red Michelin* guide for Germany and the *Varta* guide are two valuable hotel and restaurant guidebooks that can be bought in any major bookstore. They are published annually.

2. The traveler arriving in a city can get advice on accomodations and make reservations in hotels or guest houses (**Pensionen**) at tourist information offices operated by local tourist associations (**Fremdenverkehrsvereine**). These are usually located in or near the main railway station.

3. Reservations can also be made through: Allgemeine Deutsche Zimmerreservierung (ADZ), Beethovenstraße 61, 6000 Frankfurt/Main 1. Phone: (0611) 740767, Telex: 04-16666.

Guten Morgen. Ich bin gerade hier angekommen. Können Sie ein Zimmer für mich buchen?

> *Good morning. I've just arrived here. Can you book a room for me?*

Ja, natürlich. Wir haben Zimmer in Hotels, Gasthöfen und Pensionen in sechs verschiedenen Preisklassen.

> *Yes, of course. We have rooms in hotels, inns, and guest houses in six different price ranges.*

Ich möchte ein Zimmer mit Bad in einem guten Hotel.

> *I would like a room with bath in a good hotel.*

In der Kategorie II B zum Beispiel kostet eine Übernachtung mit Frühstück 40 bis 65 Mark.

In category II B, for instance, one overnight stay with breakfast costs 40 to 65 marks.

Ja, dieser Preis wäre[1] mir recht.

Yes, this price would be all right with me.

Möchten Sie im Stadt-Zentrum oder etwas außerhalb wohnen?

Would you like to stay in the center of town or somewhat outside?

Ich ziehe das Zentrum vor[2].

I prefer the center.

Dann kommen folgende Hotels in Frage: "Zum Ritter", Nummer 15 auf diesem Stadtplan, "Goldenes Lamm", Nummer 20 und "Vier Jahreszeiten", Nummer 18.

*Then you have a choice of the following hotels: "Zum Ritter" (**der Ritter** = knight), number 15 on this city map, "Goldenes Lamm" (Golden Lamb), number 20, and "Vier Jahreszeiten" (Four Seasons), number 18.*

"Zum Ritter" — das klingt so, als ob es sehr alt wäre[3].

"Zum Ritter" — that sounds as if it were very ancient.

Ja, das ist es auch. Das Haus wurde 1592 erbaut[4]. Es hat eine schöne Renaissance-Fassade mit einer Ritterfigur.

Yes, that is so. The house was built in 1592. It has a beautiful Renaissance front with a figure of a knight.

Bitte buchen Sie das Zimmer dort.

Please book the room there.

Gut, Sie bekommen gleich Ihre Bestätigung.

Very well, you'll receive your confirmation right away.

---

[1] subjunctive of **sein,** §52, here to express probability.   [2] **vorziehen,** §45.   [3] subjunctive, §54.   [4] passive voice, §50.

Es ist mir aufgefallen, daß es in vielen Städten Hotels und Gasthöfe gibt, die "Lamm", "Löwe", "Adler" oder "Drei Könige" heißen.

It has occurred to me that in many towns there are hotels and inns that are called "Lamm" (Lamb), "Löwe" (Lion), "Adler" (Eagle) or "Drei Könige" (Three Kings).

Ja, das sind Namen mit historischem oder biblischem Ursprung.

Yes, these are names with a historical or biblical origin.

Ach so ist das! Ich hatte fast gedacht, daß diese Hotels zu einer Kette gehören.

Is that so! I had almost thought that these hotels belong to a chain.

Natürlich nicht. — Hier sind noch einige Unterlagen für Sie: ein Prospekt über die Sehenswürdigkeiten der Stadt, und ein Programmheft mit den Ereignissen der Woche.

Of course not. — Here is some more material for you: a leaflet giving the interesting sights of the town and a program guide with the special events of the week.

REMARKS

Usage:

recht, right (correct)

Es ist mir recht. It is all right with me.

Er hat recht. He is right.

Ich gebe ihm recht. I admit that he is right.

in Frage kommen, to be worth considering, to be a matter of choice

nicht in Frage kommen, to be out of the question.

Im Hotel

In the Hotel

■ **Am Empfang**   *At the reception desk*

Guten Morgen. Mein Name ist Jones. Ich habe durch den
Verkehrsverein ein Zimmer reservieren lassen.
> *Good morning. My name is Jones. I had a room reserved
> through the "Verkehrsverein."*

Guten Morgen, Herr Jones. Ja, ich habe Ihre Reservierung:
Ein Einzelzimmer mit Bad für zwei Nächte.
> *Good morning, Mr. Jones. Yes, I have your reservation.
> A single room with bath for two nights.*

Richtig. Das Zimmer kostet 60 Mark pro Tag, nicht wahr?
> *Right. The room costs 60 marks per day, doesn't it?*

Ja, einschließlich Frühstück und Bedienung.
> *Yes, including breakfast and service.*

Ich hoffe, man hört den Straßenlärm nicht im Zimmer.
> *I hope one doesn't hear the street noise in the room.*

Das Zimmer ist sehr ruhig, zum Hof hin gelegen.
> *The room is very quiet, facing the courtyard.*

Darf ich Ihren Pass haben? — Bitte unterschreiben Sie das
Anmeldeformular hier.
> *May I have your passport? — Please sign the registration
> form here.*

Hat das Zimmer ein Telefon?
Does the room have a telephone?

Ja, natürlich. — Sie haben Zimmer Nummer 33. Ich lasse Ihr Gepäck sofort auf Ihr Zimmer bringen.
Yes, of course. — You have room number 33. I'll have your luggage sent to your room immediately.

REMARKS

Usage:
(sich) lassen, to let, leave; to have or cause (something done)
a. (sich) lassen + infinitive
Sie läßt sich die Haare schneiden. She is having her hair cut.
Lassen Sie bitte ein Taxi rufen. Please, have a taxi called.

In the perfect tenses, the past participle (**gelassen**) is replaced by the infinitive (**lassen**).
Er hat sich die Schuhe putzen lassen. He had his shoes cleaned.
b. Idiomatic phrases: **Lassen Sie sich Zeit.** Take your time.
Lassen Sie sich nicht stören. Don't let me disturb you.
Er läßt vielmals grüßen. He sends you many regards.
Laß mich in Ruhe! Leave me alone! **Laß das!** Stop that!
Laß uns gehen! Let's go!

..., nicht wahr? is a rhetorical question asking for confirmation. The English equivalent is an interrogative phrase, e.g., isn't it?, didn't he?
Ich habe eine Reservierung, nicht wahr? I have a reservation, don't I? **Es gibt ein Telefon, nicht wahr?** There is a telephone, isn't there?

■ **Auf dem Zimmer**   *In the room*

(Hausdiener) Hier sind Ihre Koffer, mein Herr.
(Porter) Here are your suitcases, sir.

Danke schön. — Lassen Sie bitte das Zimmermädchen kommen.

Thank you. — Please have the chambermaid come in.

(Zimmermädchen) Sie wünschen, mein Herr?

(Chambermaid) What can I do for you, sir?

Können Sie das Federbett durch eine Decke ersetzen bitte?

Can you please exchange the feather cover for a blanket?

Ja, natürlich, das läßt sich machen[5].

Yes, of course, that can be done.

Lassen Sie bitte auch diesen Anzug reinigen und die Hemden waschen.

Please also have this suit cleaned and the shirts washed.

Ja, selbstverständlich. — Stellen Sie bitte Ihre Schuhe abends vor die Türe. Sie werden vom Hausdiener geputzt.

Yes, certainly. — Please put your shoes in front of the door in the evening. They will be cleaned by the porter.

Gut. Das ist alles, danke.

O.K. That's it, thank you.

■ **Das Frühstück**   *Breakfast*

Guten Morgen, der Herr. Einmal Frühstück? Tee oder Kaffee?

Good morning, sir. One breakfast? Tea or coffee?

Guten Morgen. Ich nehme Tee. Was gibt es sonst zum Frühstück?

Good morning. I'll take tea. What else is there for breakfast?

Im Preis inbegriffen sind Brötchen, Schwarzbrot, Butter und

---

[5] §51c.

Marmelade. Hier ist unsere Frühstückskarte, falls Sie mehr bestellen möchten.

Included in the price are rolls, black bread, butter and jam.
Here is our breakfast menu, in case you want to order more.

Bringen Sie mir auch ein Glas Orangensaft und zwei Eier mit Speck.

Bring me also a glass of orange juice and two eggs with bacon.

REMARKS

Additional vocabulary: **Eier mit Schinken,** ham and eggs; **Spiegeleier,** fried eggs (sunny side up); **Rühreier,** scrambled eggs; das **Müsli,** cold cereal; der **Porridge,** der **Haferbrei,** oatmeal.

■ **Die Abreise**   *Checking out*

Ich reise morgen ab[6]. Machen Sie bitte die Rechnung fertig[6].

I am leaving tomorrow. Please have my bill ready.

Ja, selbstverständlich, Herr Jones. Soll ich Sie wecken lassen?

Yes, certainly, Mr. Jones. Shall I have you woken up?

Ja, bitte, um 8 Uhr.

Yes, please, at 8 o'clock.

* * * * * *

Guten Morgen, Herr Jones. Hatten Sie eine angenehme Nacht?

Good morning, Mr. Jones. Did you have a pleasant night?

Ja, danke. — Geben Sie mir die Rechnung bitte. Ich habe es etwas eilig.

Yes, thank you. — Give me the bill please. I am in a bit of a hurry.

---

[6] **abreisen, fertigmachen,** §45.

Hier bitte. Zwei Nächte à 60 Mark, plus Wäsche, Trocken-reinigung und Telefon. Sie können in bar, mit Euroscheck oder Kreditkarte bezahlen.

> *Here it is. Two nights, 60 marks each, plus laundry, dry cleaning, and telephone. You can pay cash, by Eurocheck, or by credit card.*

Ich bezahle mit Kreditkarte; das ist am einfachsten. Welche Karten akzeptieren Sie?

> *I'll pay by credit card; that is the easiest. Which cards do you accept?*

Wir akzeptieren alle üblichen Karten: American Express, Diners Club, Master Charge, Eurocard.

> *We accept all the usual cards: American Express, Diners Club, Master Charge, Eurocard.*

Hier ist meine American-Express Karte. — Können Sie mir bitte ein Taxi bestellen?

> *Here is my American Express card. — Can you please call a Taxi for me?*

Es steht ein Taxi vor der Tür. — Angenehme Reise, Herr Jones.

> *There is a taxi at the door. — A pleasant trip, Mr. Jones.*

■ **Word List**

die Abreise departure; checking out (of a hotel)
die Ankunft arrival
die Anmeldung registration
der Aschenbecher ashtray
die Beanstandung complaint
die Bedienung service

das Bett bed
die Bettwäsche bed linen
das Doppelzimmer double room
der Empfang, die Rezeption reception desk
der Empfangschef receptionist

der Fahrstuhl elevator, lift

das Handtuch towel

der Hausschlüssel house key

die Haustür front door

der Heizkörper radiator

die Heizung heating

die Kategorie (des Hotels) category (of the hotel)

der Kleiderbügel coat hanger

die Klingel bell

der Lichtschalter light switch

der Liegestuhl deckchair

die Lüftung ventilation

das Mittagessen lunch

der Portier bell captain

die Saison season

Hauptsaison main season

die Seife soap

der Speisesaal dining room

der Spiegel mirror

die Steckdose electric outlet

der Stecker plug

die Stromspannung voltage

das Toilettenpapier toilet paper

die Unterkunft accommodation

das Zimmer room

mit Bad with bath

mit Dusche with shower

mit fließend Kalt- und Warmwasser with hot and cold water

mit Frühstück with breakfast

mit Halbpension with breakfast and dinner

mit Vollpension with full board

mit Balkon with balcony

mit Blick auf die Berge with a view of the mountains

das Zimmermädchen chambermaid

der Zwischenstecker adapter

In der Jugendherberge

At the Youth Hostel

REMARKS

Youth Hostels offer inexpensive accommodation to young travelers in many European countries. Especially in Germany one finds them in almost every town. Many hostels are located near scenic spots; some are even installed in restored and converted castles. A guide listing Youth Hostels **(Deutsches Jugendherbergsverzeichnis)** can be bought at Youth Hostels, book stores, or from the Deutsches Jugendherbergswerk (DJH), Bülowstraße 26, 4930 Detmold.

Membership in the International Youth Hostel Federation (IYHF) is accepted in Germany. "International Guest Cards" are also issued.

Darf ich mich an euern Tisch setzen?
> *May I sit down at your table?*

Na klar, setz dich! Wir haben auch gerade unser Essen geholt.
> *Of course, sit down! We just picked up our food, too.*

Gehört ihr alle zu der Gruppe, die an der Wanderung durch Deutschland teilnimmt[7]?
> *Do you all belong to the group that is taking part in the hike through Germany?*

---

[7] relative clause, §38a.

Ja, wir haben aber nur den letzten Abschnitt der Wanderung mitgemacht. Heute sind wir hier in Überlingen[8] angekommen.

> *Yes, but we have joined only the last section of the hike. This afternoon we arrived here in Überlingen.*

Wo habt ihr angefangen?

> *Where did you start?*

In Freudenstadt[9]. Wir sind dann durch den Schwarzwald bis zum Bodensee gewandert.

> *In Freudenstadt. Then we hiked through the Black Forest to Lake Constance.*

Wann seid ihr in Freudenstadt losgegangen?

> *When did you start in Freudenstadt?*

Vor zwei Wochen. Morgen fahren wir mit dem Boot zur Insel Mainau und dann nach Konstanz[8]. Das ist unser Ziel.

> *Two weeks ago. Tomorrow we'll go by boat to the island of Mainau and then to Constance. That is our destination.*

Mit dem Boot? Und das nennt ihr Wandern?

> *By boat? And you call that hiking?*

Wir müssen unsere Kräfte schonen für das Abschiedsfest.

> *We have to save our strength for the farewell party.*

Ist jemand hier, der die ganze Tour mitgemacht hat?

> *Is anybody here who did the entire tour?*

Die zwei Jungs[10] da drüber sind vor zwölf Wochen in Flensburg[11] gestartet.

> *The two guys over there started twelve weeks ago in Flensburg.*

---

[8] town on Lake Constance.   [9] town North of the Black Forest.   [10] **Jungs** (colloq.) = **Jungen.**   [11] town at the border to Denmark.

Dafür sehen sie aber ganz munter aus. Ein neues Paar
Stiefel könnten sie beide gebrauchen.

*Considering that they look quite cheerful. They both could
use a new pair of boots.*

Und was machst du hier?

And what are you doing here?

Ich will einen Segelkurs mitmachen, der in ein paar Tagen
in der Jugendherberge in Lindau[12] anfängt.

*I want to take a sailing course that starts in a few days in
the youth hostel in Lindau.*

Es ist einfach toll, was das DJH (Deutsches Jugendherbergswerk) alles bietet! Kennt ihr das Auslandsprogramm?

It is simply super what the **DJH** *(German Youth Hostel
Federation) offers! Do you know the foreign program?*

Ja, in der Zeitschrift "Jugendherberge" hab'[13] ich es gesehen:
"Abenteuer-Urlaub in 26 Ländern.

Yes, I've seen it in the **Jugendherberge** *magazine:
"Adventure Holidays in 26 Countries."*

Ganz schön verlockend sind die Angebote: eine Wildnis-Tour
durch Grönland — mit dem Paddelboot durch Frankreich —
Mitarbeit im Kibbuz. Sogar Japan kann man sich ansehen!

*The offers are quite tempting: A wilderness tour through
Greenland — by kayak through France — work in a Kibbuz.
One can even go to see Japan.*

REMARKS

Additional vocabulary: **die Anmeldung,** registration;
die Aufnahme, admission; **der Einzelgast,** individual guest;
die Gebühr, fee; **die Gruppe,** group; **der Herbergsvater, die
Herbergsmutter,** superintendents of youth hostel; **die Koch-
gelegenheit,** cooking facilities; **die Mitgliedschaft,** membership; **der Mitgliedsausweis,** membership card; **der Schlaf-
raum,** dormitory; **der Schlafsack,** sleeping bag.

---

[12] town on Lake Constance.   [13] **hab'** = **habe.**

Restaurants

Restaurants

REMARKS

German restaurants range from luxurious places serving international dishes to fast-food diners along the Autobahn, with typical country inns serving regional specialties and establishments serving foreign food in between.

German food tends to be hearty rather than sophisticated. The wines, mostly white, have a lot of bouquet and are not expensive. The beer, especially in Bavaria, is among the best in the world.

The *Michelin* and *Varta* guides give ratings of restaurants for those with a more than passing interest in food.

■ **Zum Abendessen ausgehen**   *Going out for dinner*

Komm, laß uns heute abend zum Essen ausgehen.
Come on, let's go out for dinner tonight.

Da[14] bin ich sehr dafür. Wohin gehen wir?
I am all for it. Where shall we go?

Wir gehen in das "Jägerhaus". Du mußt endlich einmal Wild essen.
We'll go to the "Jägerhaus." You'll finally have to eat venison.

Einverstanden. Müssen wir einen Tisch reservieren?
O.K. Do we have to reserve a table?

---

[14] **da,** here used for emphasis.

Nein, an Wochentagen ist das nicht nötig.
No, that is not necessary on weekdays.

■ **Im Restaurant**   *At the restaurant*

Guten Abend, die Herrschaften[15]. — Einen Tisch für zwei Personen?
Good evening, madam; good evening, sir. — A table for two?

Ja, bitte. Ist der Tisch dort drüben frei?
Yes, please. Is the table over there free?

Ja, Sie können dort Platz nehmen. — Hier ist die Speisekarte.
Yes, you may sit down there. — Here is the menu.

■ **Die Speisekarte**   *The menu*

Ich habe nie gewußt, daß es so viele Wildspezialitäten gibt.
I've never known that there are so many game specialties.

Ich kann dir den Rehrücken mit Pfifferlingen besonders empfehlen.
I can especially recommend the saddle of roe deer with "Pfifferlinge" (a type of mushroom).

Das klingt sehr gut. Der Wildschweinbraten würde mich auch reizen.
That sounds very good. The roast of wild boar would be tempting, too.

Dann könntest Du das Menü nehmen: Tomatensuppe, Wildschweinbraten und zum Nachtisch gemischtes Eis.
Then you could take the special: tomato soup, roast of wild boar, and assorted flavors of ice cream for dessert.

[15] Formal address used for a group of two or more persons of both sexes.

Nein, das ist mir zu viel. Ich nehme den Rehrücken.
No, that is too much for me. I'll take the saddle of roe deer.

Und ich nehme das Hirschsteak. — Laß uns bestellen.
And I am taking the venison steak. — Let's order.

■ **Bestellen**   *Ordering*

REMARKS

1.   The waiter is addressed as **"Herr Ober,"** the waitress as **"Fräulein."** If the owner and his wife wait on their guests, you address them with **"Herr Wirt"** and **"Frau Wirtin."**

2.   Ice water is not served in German restaurants. In most places bread and rolls have to be ordered separately and paid for.

Herr Ober, wir möchten bestellen.
Waiter, we would like to order.

(Ober) Bitte schön, die Herrschaften?
(Waiter) May I help you?

Einmal Rehrücken und einmal Hirschsteak, bitte.
One (lit., once) saddle of roe deer and one venison steak, please.

(Ober) Und als Vorspeise?
(Waiter) And as an appetizer?

Was können Sie besonders empfehlen?
What can you especially recommend?

Der geräucherte Lachs ist ausgezeichnet. Oder möchten Sie lieber eine Suppe?
The smoked salmon is excellent. Or would you prefer soup?

Nein, geräucherten Lachs, zweimal bitte.
No, smoked salmon, two orders please.

Sehr wohl. — Möchten Sie die Weinkarte?
Very well. — Would you like the wine list?

Ja, bitte. Haben Sie einen guten deutschen Rotwein?
Yes, please. Do you have a good German red wine?

Ja, wir haben einen ausgezeichneten "Assmannshäuser",
Nummer 12 auf der Karte.
*Yes, we have an excellent "Assmannshäuser," number 12 on
the list.*

Gut, eine Flasche bitte.
Good, a bottle, please.

■ **Wie schmeckt es dir?**   *How do you like it?*

Wie schmeckt dir der Lachs mit Sahnemeerrettich?
How do you like the salmon with creamed horse-radish?

Es schmeckt sehr gut — eine ausgezeichnete Kombination.
It tastes very good — an excellent combination.

Bist Du zufrieden mit der Wahl des Restaurants?
Are you satisfied with the choice of restaurant?

Und ob! Das Lokal ist sehr gemütlich, das Essen erstklassig
und die Bedienung hervorragend.
*And how! The place is very charming, the food first class,
and the service excellent.*

Hier kommt das Wild und der Wein.
Here is the venison and the wine.

Das sieht aber gut aus[16]!
But that looks delicious!

[16] **aussehen,** §45.

Der Wein ist hervorragend! Prosit! Auf dein Wohl und auf deinen Aufenthalt in Deutschland!

> *The wine is outstanding! Cheers! Here's to your health and your stay in Germany!*

Prosit! Auf dein Wohl!

> *Cheers! Here's to you!*

REMARKS

Usage:

schmecken, to taste

Es schmeckt mir. I like it. (lit., It tastes good to me.)

Es schmeckt gut. It tastes good.

Schmeckt es dir? Do you like it?

Wie schmeckt es dir? How do you like it?

Hat Ihnen das Essen geschmeckt? Did you enjoy your food?

der **Geschmack,** taste; flavor

Sie hat einen guten Geschmack. She has good taste.

Der Wein hat seinen Geschmack verloren. The wine has lost its flavor.

gemütlich, comfortable (*chair*), cozy (*room*), sociable (*meal*)

(**Gemütlich** and its noun **Gemütlichkeit** are used very often in German. There is no exact translation into English.)

Ich mache es mir heute gemütlich. I'll take it easy today.

Machen Sie es sich gemütlich. Make yourself comfortable.

■ **Bezahlen** *Paying*

REMARKS

Usually 10% to 15% for service (**Bedienung**) and 12% value-added tax (**Mehrwertsteuer**) are included on the check. A small tip (less than 5%) is given in addition, if the service was good.

(Ober) Hat Ihnen das Essen geschmeckt?
(Waiter) Did you enjoy your food?

Es war ausgezeichnet.
It was excellent.

Darf ich Ihnen einen Nachtisch bringen?
May I serve you a dessert?

Nein danke, nur Kaffee und dann die Rechnung bitte.
No thank you, just coffee and then the check, please.

REMARKS

Besides restaurants of all types, there are a variety of places where one can find something to eat.

1. **Gasthäuser, Gasthöfe,** and **Gastwirtschaften** (local inns) usually serve standard German food and regional specialties at reasonable prices.

2. During the warm season **Biergärten** are popular places where people drink beer and eat sausages under shady trees.

3. **Ausflugslokale** are often located at scenic spots to provide food and drink to motorists and hikers. Usually they also have tables outside, and sometimes they are closed in winter. A whole musical folklore describes the happy hours spent by the easy-going Viennese drinking their **Heurigen** (new wine) on a warm summer night.

4. At a **Ratskeller** (**Rat** = *council*), located in the basement of the city hall, the city councilors used to be served what was probably the best food and drink in town. Now **Ratskellers** are open to anyone, where they still exist.

5. **Weinstuben** and **Bierkeller** are German versions of the pub. Germans prefer to take their drinks while seated — bars are a modern, cosmopolitan import. Food in these places is more in the line of snacks designed to stimulate the thirst.

6. **Schnellgaststätten** or **Imbisstuben** are German snack bars.

7. **Cafés** serve light meals in addition to cakes, coffee, and pastries.

■ Word List

die **Bedienung** service
das **Besteck** silverware
der **Brotkorb** breadbasket
die **Butter** butter
der **Essig** vinegar
die **Flasche** bottle
die **Gabel** fork
das **Gericht** dish (of food)
das **Glas** glass
die **Karaffe** decanter, carafe
der **Kellner** waiter
die **Kellnerin** waitress
der **Löffel** spoon
die **Mayonnaise** mayonnaise
das **Menü, das Gedeck** special menu, table d'hôte
das **Messer** knife
das **Öl** oil

der **Pfeffer** pepper
die **Platte** serving dish
die **Rechnung** check
die **Salatsoße** salad dressing
das **Salz** salt
die **Schüssel** bowl
die **Serviette** napkin
der **Senf** mustard
die **Speisekarte** menu
die **Tasse** cup
der **Teelöffel** teaspoon
der **Teller** plate
der **Tisch** table
das **Tischtuch** tablecloth
das **Trinkgeld** tip
die **Untertasse** saucer
der **Zahnstocher** toothpick
die **Zuckerdose** sugar bowl

Essen und Trinken

Eating and Drinking

Ich habe mich noch nicht an das warme, schwere Mittagessen in Deutschland gewöhnt.

> *I still haven't gotten used to the warm, heavy lunch in Germany.*

Das Mittagessen ist nun einmal die Hauptmalzeit des Tages hier; dafür besteht das Frühstück nur aus Brot mit Butter und Marmelade, Tee oder Kaffee.

> *Lunch happens to be the main meal of the day here; on the other hand breakfast consists only of bread with butter and jam, tea, or coffee.*

Mir erscheint das übliche Abendessen sehr knapp, weil ich gewohnt bin, später schlafen zu gehen als die meisten Deutschen.

> *To me the usual evening meal seems very skimpy, because I am used to going to bed (lit., go to sleep) later than most Germans.*

Das ist richtig. Die meisten Leute essen am Abend Brot mit Wurst oder Käse, vielleicht noch Salat oder Suppe, und gehen relativ früh ins Bett.

> *That's right. Most people eat bread and cold cuts or cheese in the evening, perhaps also salad or soup, and go to bed relatively early.*

Kaffee und Kuchen am Nachmittag ist für viele eine liebe
Gewohnheit, nicht wahr?

*Coffee and cake in the afternoon is a fond habit for many,
isn't it?*

Ja, besonders für die Hausfrauen, die oft auch Freundinnen
zum Kaffee einladen.

*Yes, especially for the housewives who often also invite girl
friends over for coffee.*

Wann trinkt man nun den berühmten deutschen Wein?

Now when does one drink the famous German wine?

Meistens nach dem Essen, wenn man mit Freunden zu
Hause oder in der Weinstube zusammensitzt.

*Mostly after dinner when one gets (lit., sits down) together
with friends at home or in a wine cellar.*

Ist das überall in Deutschland so?

Is that so everywhere in Germany?

Nein. Im allgemeinen trinkt man in Bayern und in Nord-
deutschland mehr Bier und Schnaps. Den Wein trinkt man
hauptsächlich in den Gegenden, wo er wächst: am Rhein
zwischen Bonn und dem Bodensee, am Main, am Necker und
an der Mosel.

*No. In general more beer and hard liquor are drunk in
Bavaria and Northern Germany. Wine is drunk mainly in
the regions where it grows: on the Rhine between (the city of)
Bonn and Lake Constance, on the Main, the Neckar and the
Moselle.*

REMARKS

Usage:

sich gewöhnen an, to get used to
Ich habe mich an schweres Essen gewöhnt. I got used to
heavy food.

gewohnt (*adj.*), customary
die gewohnte Arbeit, the customary job

gewohnt sein, to be used to, to be accustomed, to be wont
Ich bin das Klima gewohnt. I am used to the climate. **Ich bin gewohnt, abends wenig zu essen.** I am used to eating little in the evening.
der Mensch, human being, person
die Menschen (*pl.*), mankind, people
die Leute (*only pl.*), people

■ Vorspeisen   *Appetizers*

Aufschnitt *m.*   cold cuts
Austern *pl.f.*   oysters
geräucherter Lachs *m.*   smoked salmon
Hering *m.*   herring
Hummer *m.*   lobster
Königinpastete *f.*   pastry shell filled with meat
Krabben *pl.f.*   crayfish, small shrimp
Melone *f.*   melon

Ölsardinen *pl.f.*   sardines in oil
Räucheraal *m.*   smoked eel
Rollmops *m.*   herring roll stuffed with pickles
Russische Eier *pl.n.*   hard boiled eggs with mayonnaise and capers
Schinken   ham
Spargel   asparagus

■ Suppen   *Soups*

Bohnensuppe *f.*   bean soup
Champignonsuppe   mushroom soup
Gemüsesuppe   vegetable soup
Gulaschsuppe   goulash soup
Hühnerbrühe   chicken broth

Kraftbrühe   bouillon
Leberknödelsuppe   clear soup with liver dumplings
Nudelsuppe   noodle soup
Ochsenschwanzsuppe   oxtail soup
Tomatensuppe   tomato soup

■ Eierspeisen *Egg dishes*

gekochtes Ei *n.* boiled egg
  weich soft
  hart hard
Eier *pl.n.* **mit Schinken** ham and eggs
Eier mit Speck bacon and eggs

Omelette *n.* omelet
Pfannkuchen *m.* pancake
Rührei scrambled egg
Spiegelei fried egg (sunny side up)
verlorene Eier poached eggs

■ Fisch *Fish*

Aal *m.* eel
Barsch *m.* bass
Flunder *f.* flounder
Forelle *f.* trout
Hecht *m.* pike
Heilbutt *m.* halibut
Kabeljau *m.* cod

Karpfen *m.* carp
Muscheln *pl.f.* mussels
Sardellen *pl.f.* anchovies
Schellfisch *pl.* haddock
Seezunge *f.* sole
Thunfisch *m.* tuna

■ Wild und Geflügel *Game and fowl*

Ente *f.* duck
Fasan *m.* pheasant
Gans *f.* goose
Hähnchen *n.* chicken
Hase *m.* (European) hare (kind of rabbit)

Hirsch *m.* venison
Kaninchen *n.* rabbit
Rebhuhn *n.* partridge
Reh *n.* roe deer
Taube *f.* pigeon
Truthahn *m.* turkey

■ Fleisch *Meat*

Kalbfleisch *n.* veal
Kalbsbrust *f.* breast of veal
Kalbskotelette *n.* veal chop
Wiener Schnitzel *n.* breaded veal cutlet

Kalbsleber *f.* calf's liver
Kalbsniere *f.* calf's kidneys

Lamm *n.* lamb
Lammbraten *m.* roast lamb

Lammkeule *f.*   roast leg of
  lamb
Lammkotelette *n.*   lamb
  chop
Hammel *m.*   mutton

Rindfleisch *n.*   beef
Deutsches Beefsteak *n.*
  hamburger
gekochtes Rindfleisch *n.*
  boiled beef
Rinderbraten *m.*   roast beef
Rinderfilet *n.*   fillet of beef,
  tenderloin
Rindsrouladen *pl.f.*   beef
  rolled and stuffed

Sauerbraten *m.*   braised
  pickled beef
Steak *n.*   steak
Rinderzunge *f.*   beef tongue

Schweinefleisch *n.*   pork
(Kassler) Rippchen *n.*
  (smoked,   pickled)   pork
  ʼ chop
Schinken *m.*   ham
Schweinebraten   *m.*   roast
  pork
Schweinefilet *n.*   pork loin
Schweinekotelette *n.*   pork
  chop

■ **Wie ist das Fleisch zubereitet?**   *How is the meat*
prepared?

gebraten   fried
  im Ofen   roasted
  in der Pfanne   pan-fried,
    sauteed
  rot   rare
  halbdurch   medium
  durchgebraten   well
    done

gedämpft   steamed,
  stewed
gegrillt   grilled
gekocht   boiled
geräuchert   smoked
geschmort   braised
mariniert   marinated

■ **Beilagen**   *Side dishes*

Bratkartoffeln   *pl.f.*   fried
  potatoes
Kartoffelbrei   *m.*   mashed
  potatoes
Pommes Frites *pl.*   French
  fries

Reis *m.*   rice
Salzkartoffeln   boiled pota-
  toes
Knödel *pl.m.*   dumplings
Nudeln *pl.f.*   noodles

■ Gemüse   *Vegetables*

Blumenkohl *m.*   cauliflower
Bohnen *pl.f.*   beans
Champignons *pl.m.*   mushrooms
Erbsen *pl.f.*   peas
Grünkohl *m.*   kale
Kohl *m.*   cabbage
Kohlrabi *m.*   kohlrabi
Lauch *m.*   leeks

Mohrrüben *pl.f.*   carrots
Paprikaschoten *pl.f.*   peppers
Pilze *pl.m.*   mushrooms
Rosenkohl *m.*   Brussel sprouts
Spargel *m.*   asparagus
Spinat *m.*   spinach
Zwiebeln *pl.f.*   onions

■ Salate   *Salads*

Chicorée *m.*   Belgian endive
Endiviensalat *m.*   endive
Gurkensalat *m.*   cucumber salad
gemischter Salat *m.*   mixed salad

Kopfsalat *m.*   lettuce
rote Rüben *pl.f.*   red beets
Selleriesalat *m.*   celery salad
Tomatensalat *m.*   tomato salad

■ Obst und Nüsse   *Fruits and nuts*

Ananas *f.*   pineapple
Apfel *m.*   apple
Apfelsine *f.*   orange
Aprikose *f.*   apricot
Banane *f.*   banana
Birne *f.*   pear
Brombeere *f.*   blackberry
Erdbeere *f.*   strawberry
Haselnuß *f.*   hazelnut
Himbeere *f.*   raspberry

Johannisbeere *f.*   currant
Kirsche *f.*   cherry
Mandarine *f.*   tangerine
Mandel *f.*   almond
Melone *f.*   melon
Pfirsich *m.*   peach
Pflaume *f.*   plum, prune
Walnuß *f.*   walnut
Weintrauben *pl.f.*   grapes
Zitrone *f.*   lemon

■ Nachspeisen   *Desserts*

Eis *n.* ice cream
  gemischtes assorted
  (flavors)
Eisbecher *m.* ice cream sundae
frisches Obst *n.* fresh fruit

Fruchttörtchen *pl.n.* small
  fruit tarts
Kompott *n.* stewed fruit,
  compote
Kuchen *m.* cake
Pudding *m.* pudding

■ Alkoholische Getränke   *Alcoholic beverages*

Bier *n.* beer
  hell light
  dunkel dark
  vom Faß on tap
Likör *m.* sweet brandy, liqueur
  Aprikosenlikör apricot
  brandy
  Kirschlikör cherry
  brandy
Sekt *m.* champagne

Schnaps *m.* clear liquor
  Himbeergeist *m.* raspberry liquor
Kirschwasser *n.* Kirsch
Weinbrand *m.* brandy
Wein *m.* wine
  offen open, by the glass
  rot red
  weiß white
  süß sweet
  trocken dry

■ Alkoholfreie Getränke   *Non-alcoholic beverages*

Fruchtsaft *m.* fruit juice
Apfelsaft *m.* apple juice
Orangensaft *m.* orange
  juice
Limonade *f.* lemonade
Kaffee *n.* coffee
  mit Milch with milk
  schwarz black
  mit Sahne with cream
  koffeinfrei decaffeinated

Pulverkaffee *m.* instant
  coffee
Mineralwasser *n.* mineral
  water
Selterwasser *n.* club soda
Tee *m.* tea
  mit Milch with milk
  schwarz black
  mit Zitrone with lemon

Im Café

At the Coffeehouse

REMARKS

1.   A German **Café** should not be mistaken for an American coffeeshop. In a **Café** you can sit down, drink a cup of coffee, and relax. Nobody will rush you. Newspapers and magazines are available to the patrons. Besides pastries one can also order snacks, wine, beer, or liquor.

2.   **Konditoreien** are pastry shops that sell pastries to go. Often they also have tables and one can order coffee and choose from a wide selection of cakes, pastries, and fruit tarts with or without whipped cream.

Laß uns ins Café gehen. Ich muß etwas mit dir besprechen, und dort haben wir Ruhe.

> *Let's go to the coffeehouse. I have to discuss something with you, and there it will be quiet.*

Einverstanden, besonders da ich auch Appetit auf Kuchen mit Schlagsahne habe.

> *Agreed, especially since I also feel like having (lit. have an appetite for) pastry with whipped cream.*

Also gut. Ich lade dich ein[17]. Hier um die Ecke ist ein Café. Es hat sogar eine Terrasse.

> *O.K. I'm treating (lit., inviting) you. There is a coffeehouse around this corner. It's even got a terrace.*

---

[17] **einladen, aussuchen,** §45.

Schön, dann können wir im Freien sitzen.
Great, then we can sit outside.

Den Kuchen suchen wir hier am Buffet aus[17].
We pick out the pastry here at the counter.

Ich nehme die Mokkatorte mit Schlagsahne.
I'll take the mocha layer cake with whipped cream.

Ich will nur ein Kännchen Kaffee. Das bestellen wir am Tisch.
I only want a small pot of coffee. We order that at the table.

Der Tisch dort drüben ist frei. Setzen wir uns.
That table over there is free. Let's sit down.

Fräulein, können wir bei Ihnen bestellen.
Miss (waitress), can you take our order?

Ja, was möchten Sie?
Yes, what would you like?

Zwei Kännchen Kaffee, und die Dame hat Gebäck ausgesucht. Hier ist der Zettel.
Two pots of coffee, and the lady has picked out some pastry. Here is the receipt.

Wie angenehm es hier ist! Nun erzähl mir, was du auf dem Herzen hast.
How pleasant it is here! Now tell me what is on your mind.

REMARKS

1. Pastries: **der Kuchen,** cake, pastry; **Apfelkuchen,** apple pie; **der Apfelstrudel,** flaky pastry stuffed with apple; **Käsekuchen,** cheese cake; **Obstkuchen,** fruit tart; **Pflaumenkuchen,** plum cake; **Sandkuchen,** coffee cake; **Streuselkuchen,** cake with sugar topping.

die **Torte,** layer cake; **Mokkatorte,** coffee-flavored layer cake; **Nußtorte,** nut layer cake; **Sacher Torte,** chocolate layer cake, **Schwarzwälder Kirschtorte,** (Black Forest) cherry and whipped cream layer cake.

anderes Gebäck *n.,* other pastries; der **Keks,** cooky, biscuit; der **Krapfen,** Bismarck, doughnut; der **Lebkuchen,** gingerbread; **Makaronen** *pl.f.,* macaroons; das **Marzipan,** almond paste.

2. Usage:

etwas auf dem Herzen haben, to have something on one's mind (lit., on one's heart)

am Herzen liegen, to be important

Die Sache liegt ihr am Herzen. The matter is important to her.

3. Diminutive endings are **-lein** and **-chen.** Diminutives are always neuter and do not change endings in the plural.

die Kanne, pot; **das Kännchen,** small pot; **die Kännchen** *pl.*

das Buch, book; **das Büchlein,** small book; **die Büchlein** *pl.*

das Haus, house; **das Häuschen,** small cottage; **die Häuschen** *pl.*

Lebensmitteleinkäufe

Buying Food

REMARKS

1. Although supermarkets are becoming increasingly popular, some people still prefer to buy their food in the old-fashioned corner groceries because of the individualized service they get.

2. Open-air markets are still held in most cities and towns on certain days of the week. They add color to the street scenery, with their wide selection of flowers, fruit, vegetables, and other produce — local as well as imported.

3. **Reformhäuser** (health food stores) have quite a long tradition in Germany. The food they sell is organically grown, and chemical additives are shunned.

Guten Morgen, Frau Schmid. Was darf es heute sein?

Good morning, Mrs. Schmid. What can I do for you today?

Guten Morgen. Ich möchte gerne ein Kilo(gramm)Mehl, einen Liter Milch, ein halbes Pfund (1/2 Pfd. = 250 Gramm) Butter und ein Viertel Pfund (1/4 Pfd. = 125 Gramm) von dem Schweizer Käse.

Good morning. I would like one kilogram (2.2 lbs.) of flour, one liter (a little over a quart) of milk, half a pound of butter, and a quarter pound of the Swiss cheese.

Sonst noch etwas bitte?

Anything else, please?

Ist der Salat frisch?
Is the lettuce fresh?

Ja, wir haben ihn heute vom Großmarkt abgeholt.
Yes, we picked it up today from the central market.

Dann nehme ich noch einen Kopf Salat.
Then I'll take one head of lettuce, too.

Haben Sie gesehen der Orangensaft ist im Sonderangebot?
Die Flasche kostet zwei Mark zehn (DM 2,10) anstatt zwei
Mark dreißig (DM 2,30).
*Did you notice there is a special on the orange juice? The
bottle is two marks ten instead of two marks thirty.*

Gut, ich nehme zehn Flaschen davon[18] und zwei Flaschen
von dem Apfelsaft. Können Sie mir die Flaschen liefern?
*Good, I'll take ten bottles of that and two bottles of apple
juice. Can you deliver the bottles to me?*

Ja, natürlich, heute nachmittag. Das wär's[19] dann?
Yes, of course, this afternoon. That would be it?

Ja, das ist alles.
Yes, that's all.

Das macht im ganzen neunundzwanzig Mark sechzig (DM
29,60) bitte.
That comes to a total of twenty-nine marks sixty, please.

Brauchen Sie Kleingeld? Ich kann Ihnen einen Zwanziger
(einen 20-Mark-Schein) und neun Mark sechzig klein geben.
*Do you need change? I can give you a twenty-mark bill and
nine marks sixty in change.*

Ja, da[20] würden Sie mir einen Gefallen tun. Danke schön.
Yes, you would do me a favor. Thank you.

---

[18] pronominal compounds, §36.   [19] **wär's = wäre es.**   [20] **da,** *in this case,* here not
translatable.

REMARKS

1. Food stores: **die Bäckerei,** bakery; **das Feinkost-geschäft,** delicatessen; **das Fischgeschäft,** seafood store; **die Konditorei,** pastry shop; **das Lebensmittelgeschäft,** grocery store; **die Metzgerei, Fleischerei,** butcher shop; **das Milch-geschäft,** dairy store; **das Reformhaus,** health food store; **der Supermarkt,** supermarket; **die Weinhandlung, das Spirituo-sengeschäft,** liquor store.

2. There are many varieties of bread made of wheat **(der Weizen)** or rye **(der Roggen).** Here are a few:

das Graubrot (Mischbrot): standard German bread made from wheat and rye flour.
das Schrotbrot: made of whole rye or wheat grains that are rough-ground.
das Vollkornbrot: made of whole rye or wheat flour with whole grains added.
der Pumpernickel: heavy, dark bread made of rye with molasses added.
das Toastbrot: wheat flour bread cut into slices, similar to standard U.S. bread.
das Weißbot: wheat flour bread.

Most bread is still sold as a whole loaf **(der Laib).**

3. Sausages are a German specialty. Names differ from region to region. Here are a few basic ones:

die Blutwurst, blood sausage; **die Fleischwurst,** pork meat sausage; **die Leberwurst,** liver sausage; **die Mettwurst,** ground pork sausage; **die Schinkenwurst,** ham sausage; **die Bratwurst,** sausage for frying; **Wiener Würstchen** *pl.n.,* Frankfurters.

4. Usage:
jemandem einen Gefallen tun, to do someone a favor
Er hat mir einen großen Gefallen getan. He did me a big favor. **Können Sie mir einen Gefallen tun?** Can you do me a favor?

5

Einkäufe und Dienstleistungen

Shopping and Services

Geschäfte und Einkäufe

Shops and Shopping

REMARKS

Store hours generally are from 8 A.M. to 6:30 P.M. Many small stores close at lunchtime from 1 to 3 P.M. and on Wednesday afternoon. Stores are closed on Saturday afternoon except for the first Saturday of each month.

Erst seit ich in Deutschland lebe, fällt mir auf[1,2], wie vergeßlich ich bin.

> *Only since I have been living in Germany do I realize how forgetful I am.*

Warum ist das so?

> *Why is that so?*

Ich wollte gestern nachmittag Milch kaufen. Erst als ich vor der verschlossenen Türe des Ladens stand, fiel mir ein[1,2], daß es Mittwoch war.

> *I wanted to buy some milk yesterday afternoon. Not until I was standing in front of the locked door of the store did I remember that it was Wednesday.*

Ich verstehe; du sprichst von den Geschäftszeiten.

> *I understand; you are talking about the store hours.*

---

[1] **auffallen, einfallen,** §§45 and 60.   [2] word order in sentences introduced by subordinate clause, cf. Note to §42c.

Du hast es erraten. Neulich hatte ich Freunde eingeladen. Sie mußten Mineralwasser trinken. Weißt du warum?

> *You guessed it. The other day I had invited friends over. They had to drink mineral water. You know why?*

Ich kann es mir denken. Weil du vergessen hattest, Wein zu kaufen.

> *I can imagine. Because you had forgotten to buy wine.*

Stimmt genau. Ich hatte kurz nach 6 Uhr daran[3] gedacht. — Zu spät!

> *Exactly. I had thought of it shortly after 6 o'clock. — Too late!*

Du hättest zum Bahnhof fahren können. Es gibt dort einen Laden für Reisende, der immer auf hat.

> *You could have driven to the station. There is a store for travelers there that is always open.*

Sag mal, warum schließen die Geschäfte so früh und alle zur gleichen Zeit?

> *Tell me, why do the stores close so early and all at the same time?*

Weil die Ladenschlußzeiten durch Gesetze festgelegt sind.

> *Because the closing hours for stores are determined by law.*

REMARKS

Usage:
fallen, to fall, drop
auffallen, to be evident, to be noticeable
Es fällt ihm auf. He notices.
einfallen, to occur (to someone), to come to one's mind
Zwei Beispiele fallen mir ein. Two examples come to my mind.

---

[3] §36b.

Plötzlich fiel mir sein Name ein. Suddenly I remembered his name.

denken, to think
sich etwas denken, to imagine something
an etwas denken, to think of something

■ **Geschäfte** *Stores*

das Antiquitätengeschäft antique store
die Apotheke pharmacy
die Bäckerei bakery
das Bekleidungshaus clothing store
der Blumenladen flower shop
die Boutique boutique
die Buchhandlung bookshop
die Drogerie drugstore
das Fotogeschäft photo shop, camera store
der Friseur hairdresser, barber
das Haushaltswarengeschäft hardware store
das Hutgeschäft milliner
der Immobilien Makler real estate agent
der Juwelier jeweller
das Kaufhaus department store
die Konditorei pastry shop
der Kunsthändler art dealer
das Kurzwarengeschäft notions store

der Laden shop
das Lebensmittelgeschäft grocery store
das Lederwarengeschäft leather shop
die Metzgerei butcher
das Milchgeschäft dairy store
das Möbelgeschäft furniture store
die Musikhandlung music shop
der Obst- und Gemüseladen fruit and vegetable store
der Optiker optician
das Papierwarengeschäft stationery store
die Parfümerie drugstore
das Pelzgeschäft furrier
die Reinigung cleaner
das Reisebüro travel agency
das Schallplattengeschäft record store
das Schuhgeschäft shoe store
der Schuster shoemaker

das Spielzeuggeschäft   toy
store
das Spirituosengeschäft
liquor store
das Sportgeschäft   sport-
ing goods store
der Tabakladen   tobacco
store
das Textilgeschäft   clothing store

der Uhrmacher   watch-
maker
das Wäschegeschäft
lingerie store
die Wäscherei   laundry
die Weinhandlung   liquor
store
der Zeitungskiosk   news-
stand

In einer Boutique

In a Boutique

Ich möchte ein Kleid Größe 40 bitte.
I would like a dress in size 40, please.

Ja, bitte schön, Größe 40 ist hier drüben. Sie können die Kleider selbst durchsehen.
Yes, size 40 is over there. You can look through the dresses yourself.

Haben Sie auch noch Kleider zu reduzierten Preisen?
Do you also still have dresses at reduced prices?

Nein, der Sommer-Schlußverkauf ist vorbei.
No, the summer sale is over.

Ich möchte diese drei Kleider anprobieren bitte.
I would like to try on these three dresses, please.

Ja, nehmen Sie diese Kabine hier bitte.
Yes, take this dressing room here, please.

Das beige Kleid gefällt mir sehr gut.
I like the beige dress very much.

Es steht Ihnen ausgezeichnet. — Ich würde es aber etwas kürzen.
It looks very good on you. — I would shorten it a bit, though.

Ja, können Sie das für mich erledigen?
Yes, can you take care of it for me?

Gerne. Die Änderung kostet zehn Mark.
I'll be glad to. The alteration costs ten marks.

Gut, wann kann ich das Kleid abholen?
Fine, when can I pick up the dress?

Mittwoch, nach 10 Uhr.
Wednesday, after 10 o'clock.

REMARKS

Other useful phrases: **Das Kleid paßt dir.** The dress fits you. **Das Kleid steht dir.** The dress suits you/looks good on you. **Das Kleid ist zu knapp/zu kurz/zu weit.** The dress is too tight/too short/too wide. **Kann es geändert werden?** Can it be altered? **Der Gürtel paßt gut dazu.** The belt goes well with it. **Diese Farbe macht Sie jünger.** This color makes you look younger.

■ **Bekleidung**   *Clothing*

der Anorak   parka
der Anzug   suit
der Badeanzug   swimsuit
die Badehose   swimming trunks
der Bademantel   bath robe
die Bluse   blouse
der Büstenhalter   bra
der Gürtel   belt
die Handschuhe   gloves
das Hemd   shirt
die Hose   pants, trousers
der Hut   hat
die Jacke   jacket
das Kleid   dress
die Kniestrümpfe   knee socks
das Kostüm   suit

die Kravatte   tie
der Mantel   topcoat, overcoat
der Morgenrock   dressing gown, robe
die Mütze   cap
das Nachthemd   nightgown
der Pullover   sweater
der Regenmantel   raincoat
der Rock   skirt
der Schal   scarf
die Schürze   apron
die Socken   socks
das Sommerkleid   summer dress
die Strümpfe   stockings (women), socks (men)

die Strumpfhose   panty-
hose
das Unterhemd   under-
shirt
die Unterhose   panties
(women), underpants

der Unterrock   slip
die Unterwäsche   under-
wear, lingerie
die Windjacke   wind-
breaker

■ **Kurzwaren**   *Notions*

das Band   ribbon
der Druckknopf   snap button
der Faden   thread
das Gummiband   elastic
der Gürtel   belt
Haken *m.* **und Ösen** *f.*
hooks and eyes
der Knopf   button
die Nähnadel   needle

der Reißverschluß   zipper
die Schere   scissors
die Schnalle   buckle
die Sicherheitsnadel
safety pin
die Stecknadel   pin
das Stopfgarn   mending
yarn
das Zentimetermaß   tape
measure

■ **Materialien**   *Materials*

die Baumwolle   cotton
die Kunstfaser   synthetic
fiber
die Kunstseide   rayon
das Leder   leather

das Leinen   linen
das Nylon   nylon
die Seide   silk
das Wildleder   suede
die Wolle   wool

■ **Farben**   *Colors*

beige   beige
blau   blue
braun   brown
gelb   yellow
grau   grey
grün   green

lila   purple
rosa   pink
rot   red
schwarz   black
silbern   silver
weiß   white

■ Größen   *Sizes*

Damen   *Women*

Kleider   *dresses*

Deutschland	36	38	40	42	44	46
USA	8	10	12	14	16	18

Herren   *Men*

Anzüge   *suits*

Deutschland	46	48	50	52	54	56	58
USA	36	38	40	42	44	46	48

Hemden   *shirts*

Deutschland	36	37	38	39	41	42	43
USA	14	$14\frac{1}{2}$	15	$15\frac{1}{2}$	16	$16\frac{1}{2}$	17

In einem Schuhgeschäft

In a Shoe Store

Ich möchte ein Paar bequeme Laufschuhe haben.
I would like a pair of comfortable walking shoes.

Welche Größe brauchen Sie?
What size do you need?

Größe 5.
Size 5.

Wollen Sie Schuhe mit niedrigem Absatz oder ganz flacher Sohle?
Would you like shoes with a low heel or a flat sole?

Mit flacher Sohle bitte.
With a flat sole, please.

Wir haben diese beiden Paare zur Auswahl. Beide gibt es in braunem Leder und in Wildleder.
We have these two pairs to choose from. Both are available in brown leather and suede.

Ja, das ist was ich möchte. Ich werde sie anprobieren.
Yes, this is what I would like. I am going to try them on.

Wie passen Ihnen diese?
How do these fit you?

Sie passen ausgezeichnet. Ich nehme sie in Wildleder.
They fit very well. I'll take them in suede.

■ **Größen**   *Sizes*

Damen   *Women*

Deutschland	36	37	38	38	39	40	41
USA	6	$6\frac{1}{2}$	7	$7\frac{1}{2}$	8	$8\frac{1}{2}$	9

Herren   *Men*

Deutschland	41	42	43	44	45	46
USA	8	$8\frac{1}{2}$	$9-9\frac{1}{2}$	$10-10\frac{1}{2}$	$11-11\frac{1}{2}$	$12-12\frac{1}{2}$

REMARKS

Additional vocabulary: **Gummistiefel** *m.*, rubber boots; **Halbschuhe** *m.*, (low-heeled) shoes; **Hausschuhe,** house shoes; **Pantoffeln** *m.*, slippers; **Sandalen** *f.*, sandals; **Schuhe mit hohen Absätzen,** high-heeled shoes; **Stiefel** *m.*, boots; **Turnschuhe,** sneakers.

der Absatz, heel; **die Einlegesohle,** inner sole; **der Schnürsenkel,** shoelaces; **die Schuhkrem,** shoe polish; **die Sohle,** sole.

Im Fotogeschäft

In the Camera Store

Bitte entwickeln Sie mir diesen Farbfilm.
> *Please develop this color film for me.*

Möchten Sie auch Abzüge?
> *Would you also like prints?*

Ja, 7 1/2 × 11 cm (sieben ein halb mal elf Zentimeter).
> *Yes, 7 1/2 × 11 centimeters.*

Hier ist Ihr Beleg. Die Abzüge sind in drei Tagen fertig.
> *Here is your receipt. The prints will be ready in three days.*

Ich möchte auch noch einen 35 mm Film haben, schwarz/weiß, DIN 22, für 20 Bilder.
> *I would also like a 35 mm film, black and white, DIN 22 (ASA 125), for 20 exposures.*

Was ziehen Sie vor[4]: Kodak oder Agfa?
> *Which do you prefer: Kodak or Agfa?*

Kodak, bitte.
> *Kodak, please.*

Bitte sehr. — Ich gebe Ihnen auch ein Formular für unseren Fotowettbewerb.
> *Here it is. — I'll also give you a registration form for our photo competition.*

---

[4] **vorziehen,** §45.

REMARKS

Usage: The indirect object often has to be translated with a prepositional phrase in English, very frequently with *for*.[5]
Reparieren Sie mir diese Kamera. Repair this camera for me.
Sie reinigte ihm den Anzug. She cleaned his suit for him.
Wechseln Sie diesem Jungen den Film. Change the film for this boy.

■ Word List

der Abzug print
  Farbabzug color print
die Aufnahme, das Foto photo, picture
der Auslöser shutter release
belichten to expose
  überbelichten to overexpose
  unterbelichten to underexpose
der Belichtungsmesser exposure meter
das Bild picture
  scharf in focus
  unscharf out of focus
die Blende diaphragm
das Blitzlicht flash
der Blitzwürfel flash cube
das Diapositiv slide

entwickeln to develop
der Fotoapparat, die Kamera camera
fotografieren to photograph
der Gelbfilter yellow filter
die Kassette cartridge
körnig grainy
das Objektiv lens
das Papier paper
  glänzend glossy
  matt matte
das Stativ tripod
der Sucher viewfinder
das Tageslicht daylight
  künstliches Licht artificial light
die Vergrößerung enlargement
der Verschluß shutter

[5] cf. §40e for word order.

Im Buchgeschäft

At the Bookstore

Wo kann ich Zukunftsromane finden?
Where can I find science fiction novels?

Im ersten Stock, gleich neben der Reiseabteilung. Wir haben eine große Auswahl.
On the first floor, right next to the travel department. We have a large selection.

Haben Sie zufällig die Serie "Fantastische Bibliothek", die beim Suhrkamp Verlag erscheint?
Do you by any chance have the "Fantastic Library" series, which is published by the Suhrkamp publishing house?

Ja, sicher. Welches Buch möchten Sie?
Yes, certainly. Which book would you like?

Mir gefallen die Romane von Stanislaw Lem.
I like the novels by Stanislaw Lem.

Wir haben sein "Roboter-Märchen". Es ist gerade herausgekommen.
We have his "Robot Tale." It has just come out.

Ich habe davon gehört. Im "Spiegel"[6] war auch eine Kritik.
I've heard of it. There was also a review in the Spiegel.

---

[6] German news magazine.

Sehen Sie sich ruhig im ersten Stock um? Wir haben viele Neuerscheinungen.

> *Go ahead and browse on the second floor. We have many newly published books.*

Ich brauche auch einen Jugendherbergsführer.

> *I also need a youth hostel guide.*

Den[8] finden Sie in der Reiseabteilung.

> *You will find that in the travel section.*

Haben Sie auch Bücher in englischer Sprache?

> *Do you also have books in English?*

Ja, die Fremdsprachenabteilung ist im Erdgeschoß hinten. Dort finden Sie Bücher von amerikanischen und englischen Autoren.

> *The foreign language department is on the first floor in the rear. You'll find books by American and English authors there.*

Mich interessiert "Slaughterhouse Five" von Vonnegut. Die Handlung spielt sich doch in Deutschland ab[7]?

> *I'm interested in Slaughterhouse Five by Vonnegut. Doesn't the story take place in Germany?*

In gewissem Sinne, ja. Der Schauplatz ist Dresden im Jahre 1945. Dresden liegt heute natürlich in der DDR[9].

> *In a certain sense, yes. The scene of the action is Dresden in the year 1945. Of course, today Dresden is in the GDR.*

Danke, dann gehe ich zuerst in die Fremdsprachenabteilung.

> *Thank you, then I'll go first to the foreign language department.*

---

[7] **sich umsehen, sich abspielen,** §45.   [8] demonstrative pronouns **der, die, das,** §34.   [9] **Deutsche Demokratische Republik.**

REMARKS

1. Additional vocabulary: **das Antiquariat,** second-hand book store; **der Autor,** author; **die Belletristik,** fiction; **der Dichter,** poet; **der Klassiker,** classic; established author; **das Kunstbuch,** art book; **das Lehrbuch,** textbook; **das medizinische Buch,** medical book; **die Neuerscheinung,** new publication; **die Rezension, die Kritik** (book) review; **das Sachbuch,** non-fiction book; **der Schriftsteller,** writer; **das Taschenbuch,** paperback; **das wissenschaftliche Buch,** scientific book.

2. Usage:

erscheinen, to appear; to come out (books), to be published

sich umsehen, to look back; to browse (in a store)

interessieren, to interest
sich interessieren für, to be interested in

spielen, to play
sich abspielen, to unfold, to take place (an action)

der Schauplatz, scene of an action (in a book or play)
Der Schauplatz von Thomas Manns "Buddenbrooks" ist Lübeck. The scene of action of Thomas Mann's *Buddenbrooks* is Lübeck.

Am Zeitungskiosk

At the Newsstand

Guten Tag. Eine "Frankfurter Allgemeine"[10], bitte.
> *Good morning. A* **Frankfurter Allgemeine,** *please.*

Die ist schon weg.
> *It's sold out. (lit., It's gone already.)*

Dann geben Sie mir "Die Welt"[11]. — Ist der "Spiegel" schon da?
> *Then give me* **Die Welt.** *— Do you have the* **Spiegel** *already?*

Ja, der ist heute gekommen.
> *Yes, it's arrived today.*

Geben Sie mir den auch und eine Rolle Pfefferminz.
> *Give me that, too, and a roll of peppermints.*

Das macht zusammen vier Mark fünfzig.
> *That'll be four marks fifty altogether.*

REMARKS

1.   In addition to newspapers and magazines, newsstands often sell lottery tickets, entertainment guides, racing sheets, and small refreshments.

2.   Additional vocabulary: **die Illustrierte,** magazine;

[10] **Frankfurter Allgemeine Zeitung,** major Frankfurt newspaper.   [11] major newspaper with nationwide circulation.

die **Modezeitschrift,** fashion journal; **das Nachrichtenmagazin,** news magazine; **die Zeitung,** newspaper.

Die Anzeige, advertisement; **die Beilage,** supplement; **der Börsenkurs,** stock market quotation; **der Leitartikel,** editorial; **die Schlagzeile,** headline; **der Wirtschaftsteil,** business section.

3. Usage:

weg, fort, away; gone

Ist das Krankenhaus weit weg? Is the hospital far away?

Der Schmerz ist fort. The pain is gone. **Sie ist fort.** She is gone. **Das Geld ist weg.** The money is gone.

Im Plattengeschäft

In the Record Store

Wo ist die Abteilung für klassische Musik?
Where is the section for classical music?

Möchten Sie Platten oder Tonbänder?
Do you want records or tapes?

Eine Platte. Ich suche das Violinkonzert von Beethoven mit David Oistrakh, in Stereo.
A record. I'm looking for Beethoven's Violin Concerto with David Oistrakh, in stereo.

Sie finden die Platte im ersten Stock unter "Beethoven-Konzerte". Die Platten sind alphabetisch geordnet.
You will find the record on the first floor under "Beethoven Concerts." The records are arranged alphabetically.

Ich brauche auch eine neue Nadel. Die Ton-Wiedergabe meiner Anlage ist nicht mehr gut.
I also need a new stylus. The sound reproduction of my system is no longer good.

Das kann aber auch am Verstärker liegen.
But that can also be caused by the amplifier.

Ich glaube nicht. Wenn ich ihn an einen Empfänger anschließe, ist der Klang ausgezeichnet.
I don't believe so. If I hook it up to a receiver, the sound is excellent.

Dann ist klar, daß es nicht am Verstärker liegt. Saphir- und Diamantnadeln bekommen Sie in der Hi-Fi-Abteilung.

Then it is clear that it is not the fault of the amplifier. You get sapphire and diamond styluses in the Hi-Fi department.

REMARKS

1. Additional vocabulary: **das Album,** album; **die Aufnahme,** recording; **Höhen** *f.* **und Tiefen** *f.,* treble and bass; **der Klang,** sound; **Kopfhörer** *m.,* earphones; **der Lautsprecher,** loudspeaker; **der Netzanschluß,** circuit connection; **die (Schall)-platte,** record; **der Tonarm,** pickup arm.

2. Usage:

liegen, to lie

liegen an, to be due to, to be the fault of

Woran liegt es? What is it due to?

In der Reinigung und Wäscherei

At the Cleaners and Laundry

Ich möchte diese Sachen reinigen lassen.
I would like to have these things cleaned.

Ein Kleid, eine Hose und eine Bluse. Wann möchten Sie die Sachen abholen?
A dress, a pair of slacks, and a blouse. When do you want to pick these up?

So bald wie möglich. Ich habe auch drei Herrenhemden. Können Sie diese waschen und bügeln?
As soon as possible. I also have three men's shirts. Can you wash and iron them?

Ja, natürlich. Sie können alles zusammen am Mittwoch abholen. Hier ist Ihr Beleg.
Yes, of course. You can pick up everything on Wednesday. Here is your ticket.

Danke. Ich komme am Mittwoch morgen vorbei[12].
Thank you. I'll come by on Wednesday morning.

REMARKS

Additional vocabulary: **der Fettfleck,** grease spot; **einen Fleck entfernen,** to remove a stain; **ein Loch stopfen,** to mend a hole; **die Stärke,** starch; **der Tintenfleck,** ink spot; **der Waschautomat,** laundromat.

---

[12] **vorbeikommen,** §45.

Auf dem Postamt

At the Post Office

REMARKS

1. The **Bundespost** (Federal Postal System) not only performs normal postal services but is also in charge of the telephone and telegraph systems. It also runs interurban bus lines. The bright yellow coaches are a familiar sight in rural small towns. One can even open a savings account with the **Bundespost** and pay one's bills by drawing on it.

2. The usual postal hours are from 8 A.M. to 5 P.M. Major post offices and those located at train stations in big cities provide some services — especially operator-assisted long-distance calls — until late at night.

■ **Briefe und Postkarten**   *Letters and postcards*

Wieviel kostet dieser Brief nach USA, per Luftpost?
How much is this letter to the US by airmail?

Er wiegt etwas mehr als 20 Gramm. Das macht DM 1,50 Grundgebühr, plus 20 Pfennig[13] Luftpostzuschlag je 5 Gramm. Das sind zusammen DM 2,50.
It weighs a little more than 20 grams. That makes DM 1.50 basic charge, plus 20 pfennigs additional charge for each 5 grams for airmail. That is DM 2.50 altogether.

Was ist das Porto für diese beiden Karten nach München?
What's the postage for these two postcards to Munich?

---

[13] **20 Pfennig** refers to a sum of money, **20 Pfennige** to 20 single coins.

Je 50 Pfennig.
50 pfennigs each.

Geben Sie mir 10 Fünfzig-Pfennig-Marken bitte.
Give me 10 fifty-pfennig stamps, please.

Zehn Fünfzinger[14]. Macht zusammen DM 7.50. Bei den
Adressen fehlt die Postleitzahl.
*Ten 50-pfennig stamps. That's a total of DM 7.50. The
zip code number is missing on the addresses.*

Was ist die Postleitzahl für München?
What's the zip code number for Munich?

Schreiben Sie die Nummer 8000 vor den Namen der Stadt.
Write the number 8000 before the name of the city.

REMARKS

1. What you can do at the post office: **Briefe/Post-
karten/Pakete/Päckchen per Luftpost/Eilboten/Einschrei-
ben senden.** Send letters/postcards/packages/small packages by
airmail/express/registered mail. **Telegramme aufgeben.** Send
telegrams. **Ferngespräche anmelden.** Place long-distance phone
calls. **Rechnungen mit Zahlkarte bezahlen.** Pay bills by
money-order. **Postlagernde Sendungen abholen.** Pick up
general delivery mail.

2. Additional vocabulary: **der Absender,** sender; **das
Ausland,** foreign countries, abroad; **der Briefkasten,** mailbox;
der Briefträger, mailman; **die Drucksache,** printed matter;
der Empfänger, addressee; **die Gebühr,** fee, charge; **das Post-
fach,** post office box; **stempeln,** to stamp; **die Zollerklärung,**
customs declaration.

[14] Colloq. for 50-pfennig stamp or 50-mark bill.

■ **Telegramme**   *Telegrams*

Ich möchte ein Telegramm nach New York aufgeben.
I would like to send a telegram to New York.

Füllen Sie dieses Formular aus — alles in Großbuchstaben bitte.
Fill in this form — all in capital letters, please.

Kommt es morgen früh an[15]?
Will it arrive tomorrow morning?

Ja, Sie können es als Brieftelegramm schicken. Das ist billiger.
Yes, you can send it as a night letter. That's less expensive.

■ **Telefon**   *Telephone*

REMARKS

Phone calls to the US can be made directly by dialing first 001, then the area code of the city and the number. Rates are lower from midnight to 12 o'clock noon every day. If you cannot use a friend's phone, you'll have to go to the post office to place your call. Hotels usually charge a higher rate. For information call 0118 (domestic) and 00118 (abroad).

Ich möchte gerne ein Ferngespräch nach USA führen.
I would like to make a long-distance call to the US.

Schalter 10, bitte.
Window 10, please.

Können Sie mich mit dieser Nummer in Chicago verbinden?
Can you connect me with this number in Chicago?

---

[15] **ankommen,** §45.

Ja, gerne. Gehen Sie in Kabine 3 und nehmen Sie den Hörer ab, wenn es klingelt.

> *Yes, sure. Go to cabin 3 and take off the receiver when you hear the ring (lit., when it rings).*

Wie lange wird es dauern?
> *How long will it take?*

Die Verbindung wird sofort hergestellt.
> *The connection will be made right away.*

REMARKS

1. Useful phrases for phone conversations: **die Leitung ist besetzt.** The line is busy. **Keine Antwort.** No reply. **Bleiben Sie am Apparat, bitte.** Hold the line, please. **Kann man durchwählen?** Can one dial directly? **Ich wurde unterbrochen.** I was cut off. **Apparat 312, bitte.** Extension 312, please. **Sie sind falsch verbunden.** You have the wrong number. **Kann ich bitte Herrn Müller sprechen?** Can I please speak to Mr. Müller? **Wer ist am Apparat?** Who's calling? **Einen Moment, ich verbinde Sie weiter.** One moment, I'll transfer your call. **Er ist nicht hier.** He is not in. **Wann kommt er zurück?** When is he coming back? **Würden Sie bitte etwas ausrichten?** Would you please give him a message? **Ich rufe später noch einmal an.** I'll call again later. **Ich bin in einer Telefonzelle.** I am in a phone booth.

2. Usage: The impersonal pronoun **es** is frequently used as in English:
Es regnet. It is raining. **Es schneit.** It is snowing. **Es ist spät.** It is late.

In many cases it is rendered in English by a different construction:
Es klingelt. The bell is ringing. **Es gefällt mir.** I like it. **Es geht mir gut.** I am fine. **Sie hat es eilig.** She is in a hurry. **Sie hat es schwer.** She is having a hard time. **Bist du's[16], Karl?** Is that you, Karl?

[16] **du's = du es.**

Beim Friseur

At the Hair Stylist's

■ **Beim Damenfriseur**   *At the hairdresser's*

Guten Tag. Ich habe einen Termin bei Jean Louis.
Good morning. I have an appointment with Jean Louis.

Guten Tag, Frau Thomas. Waschen und Legen, nicht wahr?
Good morning, Mrs. Thomas. Shampoo and set, right?

Ja. Muß ich lange warten?
Yes. Do I have to wait a long time?

Nein, nur einen Moment.
No, only a moment.

* * * * * *

(Jean Louis) Guten Morgen, Frau Thomas. Ich möchte
Ihnen eine neue Frisur empfehlen. Hier auf dem Foto sehen
Sie, was ich meine.
*(Jean Louis) Good morning, Mrs. Thomas. I would like
to recommend a new hairdo to you. Here on this photo you
can see what I mean.*

Ja, gut. Diese Frisur gefällt mir.
Yes, O.K. I like this hairdo.

Ihre Dauerwellen sind noch stark genug. Bitte, nehmen Sie
dort drüben Platz zum Waschen.
*Your permanent is still tight enough. Have a seat over there
for the shampoo, please.*

Ist das Wasser recht?
> *Is the water all right?*

Können Sie es etwas wärmer[17] machen?
> *Can you make it a bit warmer?*

Ja, natürlich. Nehmen Sie einen Festiger?
> *Yes, of course. Do you take a setting lotion?*

Ja, einen roten Farbfestiger, bitte.
> *Yes, a red toning lotion, please.*

* * * * * *

Gefällt Ihnen der Schnitt?
> *Do you like the cut?*

Ja, sehr gut. Die Frisur wird kürzer[17] als[18] meine vorige, nicht wahr?
> *Yes, very much. The hairdo will be shorter than my previous one, won't it?*

Ja, richtig. Die Haare werden nicht mehr eingerollt sondern mit dem Föhn getrocknet.
> *Yes, right. The hair will no longer be put in curlers but dried with the blower instead.*

Das ist ja sehr praktisch.
> *That's very practical indeed.*

* * * * * *

Sind Sie zufrieden, Frau Thomas?
> *Are you satisfied, Mrs. Thomas?*

Ich bin mehr als zufrieden! Die Frisur ist sehr schick!
> *I am more than satisfied! The hairdo is very chic!*

---

[17] **warm, wärmer, wärmste; kurz, kürzer, kürzeste,** §20.   [18] comparison of inequality, §24.

■ **Beim Herrenfriseur**   *At the barber's*

Wie viele sind noch vor mir?
> *How many are ahead of me?*

Noch drei Herren. Mein Kollege kommt gleich wieder[19];
dann können wir zwei Kunden gleichzeitig bedienen.
> *Three gentlemen. My colleague will come back immediately;*
> *then we can take care of two customers at the same time.*

* * * * * *

Bitte nehmen Sie Platz; Sie sind jetzt dran[20]. Was darf es
sein?
> *Please take a seat; it is your turn. What can I do for you?*

Schneiden Sie mir bitte die Haare. Sie sind besonders im
Nacken zu lang.
> *Please cut my hair. It is too long, especially around the neck.*

Möchten Sie einen Messerschnitt oder einen Scherenschnitt?
> *Would you like a razor cut or a scissor cut?*

Schneiden Sie mit der Schere bitte.
> *Please use (lit., cut with) the scissors.*

Und wie kurz soll ich um die Ohren schneiden?
> *And how short do you want me to cut around the ears?*

Das Haar soll etwa zwei Zentimeter über die Ohren reichen.
Oben dünnen Sie bitte etwas aus.
> *The hair should reach about two centimeters over the ears.*
> *Please thin out (the hair) somewhat on top.*

So, das wär's. Möchten Sie eine Haarwäsche, Kopfmassage
oder Maniküre?
> *So, that's it. Would you like a shampoo, scalp massage, or*
> *manicure?*

---

[19] **wiederkommen,** §45.   [20] colloq. for **daran.**

Nein, danke, ich habe es eilig.
No, thank you, I am in a hurry.

Sie bezahlen bitte an der Kasse.
You pay the cashier, please.

Kann ich dort auch eine Packung Rasierklingen bekommen?
Can I get a package of razor blades there, too?

Ja, natürlich. Sie bekommen dort auch andere Toiletten-artikel.
Yes, of course. You can get other toilet articles there, too.

REMARKS

1. Additional vocabulary: **anfeuchten,** to moisten; **bleichen,** to bleach; **bürsten,** to brush; **die Bürste,** brush; **elektrischer Rasierapparat,** electric shaver; **färben,** to tint; **föhnen,** to blow-dry; **frisieren,** to dress (someone's) hair; **das Haarwasser,** hair tonic; **die Haube,** hairdryer; **kämmen,** to comb; **der Kamm,** comb; **die Locke,** curl; **lockig,** curly; **der Rasierapparat,** safety razor; **die Rasierseife,** shaving cream; **der Scheitel,** part (hair); **die Schuppen,** dandruff; **die Spitzen schneiden,** to trim the ends; **trockenes/fettes Haar,** dry/oily hair.

2. Usage: Note the use of the definite article and the reflexive pronoun in German where the possessive is used in English to refer to parts of one's body:[21]

Wasch dir die Haare! Wash your hair!
Er wäscht sich die Haare. He washes his hair (his own).
But: **Der Friseur wäscht seine Haare.** The barber washes his hair (someone else's).

---

[21] Cf. also Grammar §47.

Apotheke und Drogerie

Pharmacy and Drugstore

REMARKS

Pharmacies are open during regular store hours. Information about night and Sunday hours is posted at every pharmacy. Note that the typical American drugstore with soda fountain does not exist.

With some exceptions, pharmacies and drugstores are separate stores. Most pharmacies, however, have some toilet articles, and drugstores sell prescription-free drugs.

Können Sie mir etwas gegen Halsschmerzen geben?
> *Can you give me something for a sore throat?*

Diese Pillen hier sind sehr gut. Man läßt sie langsam im Mund zergehen.
> *These pills here are very good. You simply let them slowly dissolve in your mouth.*

Haben Sie auch etwas zum Gurgeln?
> *Do you also have something for gargling?*

Ja, Sie gurgeln dreimal täglich mit einem Eßlöffel voll von dieser Flüssigkeit.
> *Yes, you gargle three times daily with a spoonful of this liquid.*

Ja, das werde ich tun. — Dann möchte ich noch eine Schachtel Kleenex und eine Tube Zahnpasta.

> *Yes, I'll do that. — Then I would also like a box of Kleenex and a tube of toothpaste.*

Toilettenartikel sind dort drüben. Sie können sich selbst bedienen.

> *Toilet articles are over there. You may help yourself.*

Ich sehe die "Weleda" Zahnpasta nicht, die ich immer verwende.

> *I don't see the "Weleda" toothpaste that I always use.*

Die ist uns leider ausgegangen. Wir erwarten die Lieferung jeden Tag.

> *Unfortunately we ran out of it (lit., it has run out). We expect delivery any day.*

Dann nehme ich eine andere Marke.

> *Then I'll take another brand.*

Übrigens, wenn die Halsschmerzen nicht weggehen, gehen Sie besser zu einem Arzt.

> *By the way, if the sore throat doesn't disappear, you better go to a doctor.*

REMARKS

Useful phrases: **äußerlich anwenden,** to use externally; **innerlich anwenden,** to use internally; **vor dem Essen,** before meals; **nach dem Essen,** after meals; **in die Haut einreiben,** to rub into the skin; **die Wunde säubern,** to clean the wound; **den Verband anlegen,** to apply the bandage; **ein Rezept für die Medizin,** a prescription for the medicine.

■ **Toilettenartikel**   *Toilet articles*

der Augenbrauenstift
  eyebrow pencil
die Hautcreme cream
das Kölnischwasser
  cologne
der Lidschatten eye
  shadow
der Lippenstift lipstick
das Mundwasser mouth
  wash
der Nagellack nail polish
der Nagellackentferner
  nail polish remover
das Papiertaschentuch
  tissue

die Pinzette tweezers
der Puder powder
die Rasierklinge razor
  blade
die Seife soap
die Sonnencreme suntan
  lotion
der Spiegel mirror
die Wimperntusche mas-
  cara
die Zahnbürste tooth-
  brush
die Zahnpasta toothpaste

■ **Medikamente und Verbandszeug**   *Medicines and*
first-aid
materials

das Abführmittel laxative
die Arznei, die Medizin
  medicine
das Aspirin aspirin
die Augentropfen eye
  drops
das Beruhigungsmittel
  tranquilizer
die Binde bandage
das Heftpflaster bandaid
das Hustenmittel cough
  medicine
die Kopfschmerztablette
  headache pill

die Mullbinde gauze bandage
die Ohrentropfen ear
  drops
die Salbe ointment
die Schlaftabletten sleeping pills
die Schmerztabletten
  pain reliever
die Spritze injection
die Tropfen drops
die Zäpfchen suppositories

Beim Arzt

At the Doctor's

REMARKS

In general, doctors' offices are open from 10 A.M. to 12 noon and from 4 to 6 P.M. They are closed Wednesday afternoons, Saturdays, and Sundays. In urgent cases, if you cannot reach a doctor, you may call the **Ärztliche Notfall-Dienst** (Medical Emergency Services) or go to a hospital.

Guten Morgen. Was kann ich für Sie tun?
Good morning. What can I do for you?

Guten Morgen, Herr Doktor. Ich bin ausgerutscht und hingefallen. Mein rechtes Handgelenk tut mir sehr weh.
Good morning, Doctor. I slipped and fell. My right wrist hurts very much.

Zeigen Sie es mir bitte.
Please show it to me.

Hier. Es ist sehr geschwollen.
Here. It is badly swollen.

Ja, es sieht nicht gut aus[22]. Meine Assistentin wird sofort eine Röntgenaufnahme[23] machen.
Yes, it doesn't look too good. My assistant will take an X-ray immediately.

---

[22] **aussehen, wiederkommen,** §45.   [23] named after **Wilhelm Conrad Röntgen** who invented X-rays in 1895.

Hier ist das Bild. Sie haben Glück gehabt. Es ist nichts gebrochen.
Here is the picture. You were lucky. Nothing is broken.

Ich habe aber ziemlich starke Schmerzen, Herr Doktor.
But I have rather strong pain, doctor.

Ja, eine Verstauchung kann sehr schmerzhaft sein. Ich mache Ihnen eine Elastik-Binde um das Gelenk.
Yes, a sprain can be very painful. I'll put an elastic bandage around your wrist.

Können Sie mir etwas gegen die Schmerzen verschreiben? Ich kann nachts nicht schlafen.
Can you prescribe something for the pain? I can't sleep at night.

Ja, ich verschreibe Ihnen ein Schmerzmittel und gebe Ihnen eine Salbe zum Einreiben.
Yes, I'll prescribe a pain reliever for you and will give you an ointment.

Wie oft kann ich das Schmerzmittel einnehmen?
How often can I take the pain reliever?

Alle vier Stunden eine Pille. — Sind Sie in einer Krankenkasse?
Every four hours one pill. – Do you have health insurance?

Nein, ich bin nur zu Besuch in Deutschland. Die Rechnung bezahle ich in bar.
No, I am in Germany only on a visit. I'll pay the bill in cash.

Kommen Sie in ein paar Tagen wieder[22]. Dann kann ich sehen, ob die Schwellung fort ist.
Come back in a couple of days. Then I'll be able to see whether the swelling is gone.

REMARKS

1. Other useful phrases:
The patient: **Ich bin krank.** I am ill. **Ich fühle mich nicht wohl.** I don't feel well. I feel sick. **Ich habe Fieber.** I have a fever. **Ich habe mich erkältet.** I've caught a cold. **Ich habe Magenbeschwerden.** My stomach is upset. **Mir ist übel.** I feel sick/nauseous.
The doctor: **Machen Sie sich bitte frei.** Undress, please. **Öffnen Sie den Mund.** Open your mouth. **Husten Sie.** Cough. **Atmen Sie tief.** Breathe deeply. **Tut das weh?** Does that hurt? **Es ist nichts Ernstes.** It's nothing serious.

2. Usage:
das **Glück,** luck; das **Pech,** bad luck
Glück haben, to be lucky; **Viel Glück!** Good luck!
glücklich sein, to be happy

■ **Körperteile und Funktionen**   *Body parts and functions*

der Arm arm	**das Gehirn** brain
die Atmung breathing, respiration	**das Gelenk** joint
das Auge eye	**das Gesicht** face
das Augenlid eyelid	**der Hals** neck, (inside) throat
der Bauch abdomen	**die Hand** hand
das Bein leg	**das Handgelenk** wrist
die Blase bladder	**die Haut** skin
der Blinddarm appendix	**das Herz** heart
das Blut blood	**die Hüfte** hip
der Blutdruck blood pressure	**der Kiefer** jaw
die Brust breast, chest	**das Kinn** chin
der Daumen thumb	**das Knie** knee
der Ellbogen elbow	**der Knöchel** ankle
die Ferse heel	**der Knochen** bone
der Finger finger	**der Kopf** head
der Fuß foot	**der Körper** body
	der Kreislauf circulation

die **Leber** liver
die **Lippe** lip
die **Lunge** lung
der **Magen** stomach
die **Mandeln** tonsils
der **Mund** mouth
der **Muskel** muscle
der **Nagel** nail
die **Nase** nose
der **Nerv** nerve
die **Niere** kidney
das **Ohr** ear
die **Rippe** rib
der **Rücken** back
die **Schläfe** temple

der **Schenkel** thigh
das **Schlüsselbein** collar-
  bone
die **Schulter** shoulder
die **Stirn** forehead
der **Stuhlgang** bowel
  movement
der **Urin** urine
die **Vene** vein
die **Verdauung** digestion
die **Wirbelsäule** spine
der **Zahn** tooth
das **Zahnfleisch** gums
die **Zehe** toe
die **Zunge** tongue

■ **Krankheiten**   *Diseases*

die **Allergie** allergy
der **Anfall** attack, fit
das **Asthma** asthma
der **Ausschlag** rash
die **Blinddarmentzündung**
  appendicitis
die **Bronchitis** bronchitis
die **Diabetes** diabetes
der **Durchfall** diarrhea
die **Entzündung** inflam-
  mation
das **Erbrechen** vomiting
die **Erkältung** cold
das **Fieber** fever
das **Geschwür** ulcer
die **Grippe** flu
die **Halsschmerzen** sore
  throat

der **Herzfehler** cardiac
  condition
der **Heuschnupfen** hay
  fever
der **Husten** cough
der **Knochenbruch** frac-
  ture
der **Krampf** cramp
die **Lebensmittel-Vergif-
  tung** food poisoning
die **Mandelentzündung**
  tonsillitis
die **Magenschmerzen**
  stomach pains
die **Migräne** migraine
die **Ohrenschmerzen** ear-
  ache
die **Quetschung** bruise

das Rheuma rheumatism
die Schlaflosigkeit insom-
nia
**der Schmerz, die Schmer-
zen** *pl.* pain
der Schnupfen cold
die Schwellung swelling
der Sonnenbrand sunburn
die Übelkeit nausea

die Verdauungsstörung
indigestion
die Vergiftung poisoning
die Verletzung injury
die Verstauchung sprain
die Verstopfung constipa-
tion
die Wunde wound

■ **Ärztliche Spezialisten** *Medical specialists*

der Augenarzt eye specialist, ophthalmologist
der Chirurg surgeon
der Frauenarzt gynecolo-
gist
**der Hals-, Nasen- und Oh-
renarzt** ear, nose, and
throat specialist
der Hautarzt dermatolo-
gist
der Internist internist

der Kinderarzt pediatri-
cian
der Nervenarzt neurolo-
gist
der Orthopäde ortho-
pedist
der Praktische Arzt general practitioner
der Psychiater psychia-
trist

Beim Zahnarzt

At the Dentist's

(Sprechstundenhilfe) Waren Sie schon einmal bei uns?
(Assistant) Have you been here once before?

(Patient) Nein, noch nicht.
(Patient) No, not yet.

Geben Sie mir bitte Ihren Krankenschein.
Give me your health insurance form, please.

Hier, bitte.
Here it is.

Danke. Ich brauche noch Ihre Telefonnummer.
Thank you. I also need your telephone number.

Die Nummer ist 801214.
The number is 801214.

Sie können jetzt im Wartezimmer Platz nehmen.
You can now take a seat in the waiting room.

* * * * * *

(Zahnarzt) Bitte, machen Sie es sich bequem. Haben Sie
Schmerzen?
*(Dentist) Please, make yourself comfortable. Do you have
any pain? (lit., pains)*

Nein, ich habe keine Schmerzen. Ich habe eine Füllung
verloren, unten links.
*No, I have no pain. I have lost a filling, on the bottom left
side.*

Öffnen Sie den Mund bitte. — Alles klar. Ich kann Ihnen sofort eine neue Füllung machen.

Open your mouth, please. — Everything is fine. I can put in a new filling for you right away.

Hoffentlich brauchen Sie mir keine Spritze zu geben.

I hope you don't need to give me a shot.

Nein, Sie werden kaum etwas spüren. Ich brauche nicht in der Nähe des Nervs zu bohren.

No, you will hardly feel anything. I don't need to drill close to the nerve.

Das freut mich.

I'm glad.

* * * * * *

So, bitte wieder spülen. — War es schlimm?

Finished, rinse again please. — Was it bad?

Nein, es hat kaum weh getan.

No, it hardly hurt.

Und nun die Füllung. Bitte beißen Sie leicht zu.

And now the filling. Please bite down on your teeth lightly.

Es fühlt sich gut an.

It feels good.

Schön. Bitte essen Sie eine Stunde lang nichts.

Fine. Please don't eat anything for one hour.

REMARKS

Additional vocabulary: **der Backenzahn,** molar; **betäuben,** to anesthetize, **örtliche Betäubung,** local anesthetic; **die Brücke,** bridge; **die Krone,** crown; **künstliches Gebiß,** denture; **das Loch,** cavity; **der Schneidezahn,** incisor; **der Zahn,** tooth; **einen Zahn ziehen,** to pull a tooth; **das Zahnfleisch,** gums; **Zahnschmerzen** *m.,* toothache.

6

Unterhaltung und Sport

Entertainment and Sports

Kino und Theater

Movies and Theater

■ **Kino**   *Movies*

Ich würde gerne heute abend ins Kino gehen.
> *I'd like to go to the movies tonight.*

Welchen Film willst du sehen?
> *Which picture do you want to see?*

Im Studio 1 zeigen sie Chaplin-Filme diese Woche.
> *At Studio 1 they are showing Chaplin films this week.*

Oh, das ist prima. Welcher Film spielt heute abend?
> *Oh, that's great. Which film are they showing tonight?*

"Moderne Zeiten." Ich würde den Film gerne noch einmal sehen.
> *"Modern Times." I'd love to see that movie again.*

Ich auch. Wann fängt die Abendvorstellung an[1]?
> *Me too. When does the evening performance start?*

Um 8 Uhr. Wir brauchen nicht pünktlich zu sein, weil vorher Reklame gezeigt wird.
> *At 8 o'clock. We don't need to be punctual because they show commercials first.*

Ich bin nicht so sicher. Es könnte ausverkauft sein.
> *I am not so sure. It could be sold out.*

---

[1] **anfangen,** §45.

Du hast recht. Laß uns rechtzeitig gehen.
You are right. Let's go on time.

■ **Theater**   *Theater*

REMARKS

Repertory theaters are found in almost every medium-sized German town. They are usually run by local or state governments and offer plays, musicals, and, frequently, even operas.

Laß uns nächstes Wochenende ins Theater gehen.
Let's go to the theater next weekend.

Du möchtest gerne das Dürrenmatt-Stück[2] sehen, nicht wahr?
You would like to see the play by Dürrenmatt, wouldn't you?

Ja, die Kritik war sehr gut.
Yes, the review was very good.

Wie heißt das Stück noch?
What's the title of the play again?

"Der Besuch der alten Dame."
"The Visit of the Old Lady."

Gut, ich werde zwei Karten für Freitag besorgen.
O.K., I'll get two tickets for Friday.

* * * * * *

Bitte zwei Karten für Freitag abend.
Please two tickets for Friday evening.

Wir haben nur noch erstes und zweites Parkett. Die Ränge und Logen sind ausverkauft.
We have only first and second orchestra left. The balconies and boxes are sold out.

[2] **Friedrich Dürrenmatt,** contemporary Swiss author and playwright.

Wie teuer ist das zweite Parkett?
How much is the second orchestra?

Fünfzehn Mark die Karte.
Fifteen marks each ticket.

Gut. Geben Sie mir zwei Karten, wenn möglich in der Mitte.
O.K. Give me two tickets, if possible in the center.

Ich kann Ihnen zwei Karten in der zwölften Reihe geben, Plätze 349 and 350.
I can give you two tickets in the twelfth row, seats 349 and 350.

* * * * * *

Willst du deinen Mantel in der Garderobe lassen?
Do you want to leave your coat in the cloakroom?

Ja, gerne. Zu welchem Eingang müssen wir gehen?
Yes, I'd like to. To which entrance do we have to go?

Links, zweites Parkett.
Left, second orchestra.

(Platzanweiserin)³ Darf ich Ihre Karten sehen?
(Usher) May I see your tickets?

Hier, bitte. Kann ich ein Programm haben?
Here they are. Can I have a program?

Ja, bitte schön. Dort sind Ihre Sitze.
Yes, here you are. There are your seats.

* * * * * *

Die Pause dauert 20 Minuten. Hast du Durst?
The intermission is going to last 20 minutes. Are you thirsty?

Ja, laß uns an die Bar gehen. — Wie gefällt dir das Stück?
Yes, let's go to the bar. — How do you like the play?

---

³ female usher.

Es ist eine hervorragende Inszenierung.
It is an excellent production.

Es ist eben auch ein spannendes Stück.
It is after all a thrilling play.

Du hast recht, aber auch die Besetzung ist sehr gut.
You are right, but the cast is very good, too.

Diesmal haben die Kritiker völlig recht gehabt.
This time the critics were completely right.

REMARKS

1. Additional vocabulary: **das Ballet,** ballet; **die Bühne,** stage; **das Bühnenbild,** stage setting; **die Tragödie,** tragedy; **die Handlung,** plot; **der Kartenvorverkauf,** advance ticket sale; **die Kasse,** box office; **die Komödie,** comedy; **einen Platz reservieren,** to reserve a seat; **der Regisseur,** director; **die Rolle,** part; **das Schauspiel,** drama; **der Schauspieler,** actor; **die Schauspielerin,** actress; **der Vorhang,** curtain; **die Vorstellung,** show, performance.

2. Usage:
eine Rolle spielen, to play a part (role)
Anthony Quinn spielte die Rolle des Alexis Sorbas. Anthony Quinn played the role of Alexis Sorbas. **Neid spielte eine Rolle in ihrer Einstellung.** Envy played a role in her attitude.

Durst/Hunger/Furcht/Lust haben, to be thirsty/hungry/afraid/eager.

Musik und Festspiele

Music and Festivals

REMARKS

Instrumental music has a very long and rich tradition in Germany that goes back to the Middle Ages. It is probably the art form in which Germany has excelled the most, and names like Bach, Beethoven, Mozart, Schubert, Wagner, and Hindemith are household words around the world.

Concert music was an indispensable part of court life up through the eighteenth century. This rich heritage is still alive today in the many orchestras, ballets, concerts, and music festivals sponsored by cities and local governments. Public subsidies, paid by the tax payer, generously support music, theater, and the arts in general, giving them to some extent a traditional and established flavor.

Ich werde mir morgen die "Matthäus Passion"[4] in der Peterskirche anhören.

> *I am going to listen to the "St. Matthew Passion" in the Peterskirche (St. Peter's Church) tomorrow.*

Da hast du eine gute Wahl getroffen.

> *There you've made (lit., hit upon) a good choice.*

Die Wahl fällt schwer, denn es ist hier sehr viel los auf dem Gebiet der Musik.

> *The choice is difficult, since there is a lot going on in the field of music here.*

---

[4] by **Johann Sebastian Bach,** 1685–1750.

Ja, die Musik hat in Deutschland immer eine große Rolle gespielt.

Yes, music has always played an important part in Germany.

Kannst du mir einiges darüber erzählen?

Can you tell me something about it?

Ja, natürlich. Es waren hauptsächlich die Fürsten, die zur Zeit Bachs die Künste gefördert haben.

Yes, of course. At the time of Bach, it was mainly the princes who sponsored the arts.

Und für wen hat Bach seine Musik geschrieben?

And for whom did Bach write his music?

Er ist viel gereist. Er hat zum Beispiel die "Brandenburgischen Konzerte" für Friedrich den Großen[5] von Preußen geschrieben.

He traveled a lot. For example, he wrote the "Brandenburg Concertos" for Frederick the Great of Prussia.

Händel[6] war auch an einem deutschen Fürstenhof, bevor er nach England ging, nicht wahr?

Händel was also at a German court before he went to England, wasn't he?

Ja, er war in Herrenhausen bei Hannover, der Sommerresidenz der Welfen[7].

Yes, he was in Herrenhausen close to Hanover, the summer residence of the Welfen.

Beide Komponisten haben aber auch Kirchenmusik geschrieben.

But both composers also wrote church music.

---

[5] 1712–1786.   [6] **Georg Friedrich Händel,** 1685–1759.   [7] Ruling house of the German state of Hanover. In 1714 the ruler of Hanover became King of England as George I.

Ja, sie schrieben Tafelmusik für die Höfe und Orgel- und Chormusik für die Kirchen.

Yes, they wrote dinner music for the courts and organ and choir music for the churches.

Dann muß man natürlich auch Ludwig II. von Bayern[8] und Richard Wagner[9] erwähnen.

Then, of course, one has to mention Ludwig II of Bavaria and Richard Wagner.

Von dieser Verbindung habe ich schon gehört.

I have already heard of this connection.

Wagners "Tristan" wurde 1865 im Nationaltheater in München uraufgeführt.

Wagner's "Tristan" had its original premiere at the Nationaltheater in Munich in 1865.

Da du Wagner erwähnst: Zu den Festspielen nach Bayreuth würde ich auch gerne gehen.

Since you mention Wagner: I'd love to go to Bayreuth to the festival, too.

Viele Festspiele und Konzerte in alten Schlössern bringen uns die Vergangenheit etwas näher[10].

Many festivals and concerts in old castles and churches bring the past somewhat closer to us.

Aber die Tradition wird auch in moderner Umgebung fort-geführt, wie in der Berliner Philharmonie.

But tradition is continued also in modern surroundings, as in the Berliner Philharmonie.

---

[8] King of Bavaria, 1845–1886.   [9] 1813–1883.   [10] **näherbringen,** §45.

Ja, in diesem hochmodernen Gebäude dirigiert an einem
Abend Karajan die Berliner Philharmoniker, und an einem
andern Abend geben die Rolling Stones ein Gastspiel.

*Yes, in this highly modern building Karajan conducts the
Berlin Philharmonics on one evening, and on another evening
the Rolling Stones give a guest performance.*

REMARKS

1. Additional vocabulary: **der Dirigent,** conductor; **die
Kammermusik,** chamber music; **die klassische/moderne
Musik,** classical/modern music; **komponieren,** to compose; **der
Komponist,** composer; **das Konzert,** concert; **der Konzertsaal,**
concert hall; **musizieren,** to play music; **der Musiker,** musician;
die Oper, opera; **das Orchester,** orchestra; **der Solist,** soloist;
die Symphonie, symphony.

die Flöte, flute; **die Geige,** violin; **die Klarinette,**
clarinet; **das Klavier,** piano; **die Trommel,** drum; **die Trom-
pete,** trumpet.

2. Usage:

los, loose

ein loser Knopf, a loose button; **Die Schraube ist los.** The screw
is loose.

loswerden, to get rid of

Sie wollte ihren Mann loswerden. She wanted to get rid of her
husband. **Er wurde sein Geld in der Bar los.** He got rid of his
money in the bar.

losgehen, to leave, start, begin

Das Spiel geht los. The game begins.

Idiomatic phrases: **In der Stadt ist viel los.** A lot is going on in town.
Was ist los? What's going on?

When **es** (or **das**) is used with **sein** and the real subject is a noun or
personal pronoun, the form of **sein** agrees with the noun or pronoun.
Ich bin es (bin's). It's me. **Du bist es!** It is you! **Es klingelt.**
Das sind unsere Freunde. The bell is ringing. It's our friends.

Museen und Galerien

Museums and Galleries

REMARKS

The historic diversity of Germany is responsible for the wide dispersal of museums, art treasures, and important galleries throughout the country. Many small and medium-sized towns have inherited the rich artistic treasures that their former rulers once accumulated. The federal structure of the present-day **Bundesrepublik** favors the retention of this decentralized art scene.

Ich will mir diese Woche die Museen hier in Kassel ansehen.
> *I want to have a look at the museums here in Kassel this week.*

Dabei wirst du auch einiges über die Geschichte unserer Stadt erfahren.
> *In the process (lit., thereby) you will also find out something about the history of our town.*

Du sprichst wahrscheinlich von euren früheren Landesherren, den Markgrafen von Hessen-Kassel?
> *You are probably talking about your former sovereigns, the Margraves of Hessen-Kassel?*

Ganz richtig.
> *Quite right.*

Ich weiß schon einiges über diese Herren: Landgraf Friedrich
II.[11] hat 12.000 seiner Untertanen an die Engländer ver-
mietet.

> *I already know something about these gentlemen: one of them,
> Landgrave Frederick II, hired out 12,000 of his subjects to
> the British.*

Ja, sie haben in den amerikanischen Freiheitskriegen als
Söldner gekämpft.

> *Yes, they fought as mercenaries in the American War of
> Independence.*

Er hat wohl Geld für seine kostspieligen Bauprojekte ge-
braucht.

> *He probably needed money for his costly building projects.*

Genauso war es. Er verwendete das Geld zum Beispiel für
das Friedericianum, das er für seine Kunstsammlung und
Bibliothek bauen ließ.

> *That's exactly how it was. He used the money, for example,
> for the Friedericianum, which he ordered built for his art
> collection and library.*

Findet dort nicht alle vier Jahre die "documenta"[12] statt[13]?

> *Isn't that where the "documenta" takes place every four
> years?*

Ja, ein großer Teil der Bilder und Skulpturen werden dort
ausgestellt.

> *Yes, a large number of the pictures and sculptures are exhibited
> there.*

Hat Friedrich II. auch die heutige Staatliche Gemäldegalerie
gegründet?

> *Did Frederick II also found the present-day State Picture
> Gallery?*

---

[11] 1760–1785.   [12] important international modern art exhibition.   [13] **stattfinden,**
to take place, §§45 and 60.

Nein, das war Landgraf Wilhelm VIII.,[14] sein Vorgänger.
No, that was Landgrave William VIII, his predecessor.

Ich habe gelesen, daß die Sammlung bei seinem Tod 869 Gemälde umfaßte.
I read that at his death the collection comprised 869 paintings.

Man muß gestehen, daß der Landgraf einen äußerst guten Geschmack besaß[15]: Er kaufte bedeutende Gemälde von Holbein, Rubens, Rembrandt, van Dyck, Dürer, Cranach, Tizian und anderen Künstlern.
One has to admit that the landgrave had (lit., possessed) excellent (lit., extremely good) taste: He bought important paintings by Holbein, Rubens, Rembrandt, van Dyck, Dürer, Cranach, Titian, and other artists.

Die Staatliche Gemäldegalerie befindet sich heute im Schloß Wilhelmshöhe, nicht wahr?
The State Picture Gallery is now in Wilhelmshöhe Castle, isn't it?

Ja, und auch eine interessante Antikenabteilung.
Yes, and also an interesting department of antiquities.

Ich habe im Prospekt gelesen, daß es auch ein Naturkundemuseum, ein Brüder-Grimm-Museum[16] und ein Deutsches Tapetenmuseum gibt.
I read in the brochure that there is also a Museum of Natural History, a "Brothers Grimm Museum," and a German Wallpaper Museum.

Ja, das Naturkundemuseum ist im Ottoneum untergebracht, einem schönen Renaissancebau.
Yes, the Museum of Natural History is housed in the Ottoneum, a beautiful Renaissance building.

---

[14] 1730–1760.   [15] **besitzen, besaß, besessen.**   [16] **Brüder Grimm:** 19th-century writers and collectors of German fairy tales.

Ich werde auf den Spuren der Landgrafen bestimmt eine interessante Woche verbringen.

I will certainly spend an interesting week in the footsteps of the Landgraves.

REMARKS

Art periods and styles: **die Antike,** antiquity; **das Mittelalter,** Middle Ages; **die Romanik,** Romanesque style; **die Gotik,** Gothic style; **die Renaissance,** Renaissance; **der Barock,** baroque style; **der Klassizismus,** classicism; **die Romantik,** romanticism; **der Impressionismus,** impressionism; **die moderne Kunst,** modern art; **der Expressionismus,** expressionism; **die abstrakte Kunst,** abstract art.

Ein Abend in Heidelberg

A Night Out in Heidelberg

Schön, wieder mal im "Sole D'oro" zu sein. Die haben das beste italienische Essen in der Stadt.

> *Nice to be at the "Sole D'oro" again. They've got the best Italian food in town.*

Und gemütlich ist es auch mit all den Bildern von Heidelberger Malern an den Wänden. — Was machen wir nach dem Essen?

> *And it is a cozy place with all the pictures by Heidelberg painters on the walls. — What are we going to do after dinner?*

Willst du in eine Studentenkneipe[17] oder in eine Diskothek gehen?

> *Do you want to go to a student pub or a discoteque?*

Eigentlich habe ich Lust zum Tanzen. Du auch.

> *Actually I feel like dancing. You too?*

Ja. Wollen wir ins "Cave" gehen?

> *Yes. Shall we go the "Cave"?*

Das ist immer so voll. Ich finde den "Club 1900" besser.

> *That is always so crowded (lit., full). I find the "Club 1900" better.*

---

[17] **Kneipe,** colloq. for **Lokal = pub.**

Also nein, dann gehe ich schon lieber in die "Katakombe".
Die haben immer die neuesten Hits.

> *Oh no, then I rather go to the "Katakombe." They always
> have the latest (lit., newest) hits.*

Was gibt es sonst noch?

> *What else is there?*

Sonst fällt mir nur noch der "Oldtimer-Club" ein[18].

> *The only other place that comes to mind is the "Oldtimer Club."*

Weißt du was, wir ziehen einfach los[18] und bleiben da, wo es
uns gefällt.

> *You know what, let's simply take off and stay where we like it.*

Gute Idee. Laß uns gehen.

> *Good idea. Let's go.*

Es ist ein schöner Abend. Wir könnten vorher am Neckar
spazierengehen.

> *It's a nice evening. We could first go for a walk along the
> Neckar River.*

Sag mal, ist heute nicht Schloßbeleuchtung und Feuerwerk?

> *Tell me, don't they have castle illumination and fireworks
> today?*

Ja, du hast recht. Von der Alten Brücke können wir das
Feuerwerk am besten sehen.

> *Yes, you are right. From the "Old Bridge" we can see the
> fireworks best.*

Und danach bummeln wir durch die Altstadt und gehen in
eine Diskothek.

> *And after that we'll stroll through the old city and go to a
> discoteque.*

---

[18] **einfallen, losziehen,** §45.

Fußball im Fernsehen

Soccer on Television

■ **Das Fußballspiel**   *The soccer game*

REMARKS

Fußball, or soccer, which is not to be confused with American football, enjoys the same popularity in Germany as football and baseball combined in the United States. On Saturdays, when the important games are played, thousands root for their home teams in the large stadiums or watch them, glued to their television sets.

Professional teams with names like **Borussia Dortmund** and **Eintracht Frankfurt** are grouped into several **Ligen** (leagues), of which the **Bundesliga** is the most prestigious one. In international competition the Bundesrepublik counts among the leaders: in 1972 the national team won the European championship and in 1974 the world championship.

However, **Fußball** is also a popular participation sport; almost every small town or village boasts an amateur club.

Ich habe für das Spiel FC Köln gegen Nottingham Forest keine Karten mehr bekommen. Es ist das Halb-Finale um den Europa-Cup, und die Karten waren schnell ausverkauft.

I haven't been able to get tickets for the FC-Köln–Nottingham Forest game. It's the semi-finals for the Europa Cup, and the tickets were sold out quickly.

Schade. Ich hätte gern einmal ein Fußballspiel gesehen.

What a pity. I would have liked to see a soccer game once.

Das ist nicht so schlimm. Sehen wir es uns im Fernsehen an[19]. Das Spiel wird am Samstag direkt vom Stadion in Köln übertragen.

It doesn't matter. Let's look at it on the TV. The game will be transmitted directly from the stadium in Cologne on Saturday.

In Farbe?

In color?

Ja, im 1. Programm.

Yes, on Channel 1.

Erkläre mir bitte ein bißchen die Spielregeln.

Please explain the rules of the game to me briefly.

Jede Mannschaft spielt mit elf Spielern, und zwar mit einem Torwart, vier Abwehrspielern, zwei Mittelfeldspielern und vier Stürmern. Der Ball darf nicht mit den Händen oder Armen absichtlich berührt werden.

Each team plays with eleven players, namely with one goalkeeper, four fullbacks, two halfbacks, and four forwards. The ball must not be touched intentionally with the hands or arms.

Vom Torwart auch nicht?

Not even by the goalkeeper?

Doch, der darf ihn mit den Händen fangen. Es ist auch wichtig, daß die Spieler sich nicht gegenseitig[20] zu Fall bringen dürfen.

Yes, he is allowed to catch it with his hands. It is also important that the players are not allowed to tackle each other (lit., to make each other fall down).

---

[19] **ansehen, wegnehmen, losgehen, anstellen,** §45.   [20] §47c.

Wie nehmen sie sich dann gegenseitig den Ball weg?
How then do they take the ball away from each other?

Der Ball muß mit viel Geschick dem Gegner vor den Füßen weggestoßen werden.
The ball has to be skillfully kicked away from the opponent's feet.

Wie lange dauert ein Spiel?
How long does a game last?

Zwei Perioden von je 45 Minuten. Du wirst sehen, Fußball ist für den Zuschauer kein kompliziertes Spiel.
Two periods of 45 minutes each. You will see, soccer is not a complicated game for the spectator.

■ Am Fernseher   *In front of the TV set*

REMARKS

In Germany, television and radio are operated by public, independent, non-profit corporations that are financed by fees charged to owners of television sets or radios. There are three different TV programs, two of which are the same throughout the country, while the third program is different from region to region. Heavy emphasis is placed on news, current events, sports, and cultural features. Entertainment programs, especially crime thrillers and Westerns, are often American productions.

Du bist früh da. Das Spiel geht erst in etwa einer halben Stunde los[19].
You are early. The game will start only in about half an hour.

Es war viel weniger Verkehr als gewöhnlich.
There was much less traffic than usual.

Machen wir es uns gemütlich. Ich habe auch Bier kalt gestellt.

> *Let's be comfortable (lit., make it comfortable for ourselves).*
> *I have put some beer in the refrigerator (lit., I have put some beer in the cold).*

Was gibt es denn sonst noch im Fernsehen?

> *What else is there on television?*

Im 2. Programm wird gerade die Muppets-Show gezeigt.

> *On Channel 2 they are just showing the Muppets Show.*

Stell es mal an[19]. Ich würde auch gern die Reklame sehen.

> *Why don't you turn it on. I'd also like to see the commercials.*

Die gibt es nicht während des Programms, sondern nur zu bestimmten Zeiten.

> *There is none during the program, but only at certain times.*

Dann wird auch das Fußballspiel nicht unterbrochen?

> *Then the soccer game will also not be interrupted?*

Nein, bis zur Pause gibt es keine Unterbrechung.

> *No, there will be no interruption until the intermission.*

REMARKS

1. Additional sports vocabulary: **das Boxen,** boxing; **das Eishockey,** ice hockey; **das Fechten,** fencing; **das Fischen,** fishing; **das Jagen,** hunting; **der Handball,** handball; **das Radfahren,** cycling; **das Reiten,** horseback riding; **das Schlittschuhlaufen,** skating; **das Schwimmen,** swimming; **das Segeln,** sailing, **das Skilaufen,** skiing; **das Tennis,** tennis; **das Turnen,** gymnastics; **das Wandern,** hiking.

das Ergebnis, score; **gewinnen/verlieren,** to win/lose; **der Trainer,** coach.

2. Usage:

(Es ist) schade, it is a pity

(Es ist) schade, daß er nicht kommen kann. It is a shame that he can't come.

schlimm, bad, disagreeable — **schlecht,** bad, of poor quality
Die Wunde ist schlimm. The wound is bad.
Das Programm ist schlecht. The program is bad.

"Schlimm" refers more to an unpleasant or dangerous conse-
quence, **"schlecht"** more to a quality.
Idiomatic use: **Das ist nicht schlimm. Das macht nichts.** It
doesn't matter.

dürfen, to be allowed to
Du darfst das nicht tun. You are not allowed to do that./You
must not do that.
But:
Er mußte das nicht tun. He did not have to do that.

Tennis

Tennis

Die Sonne scheint. Laß uns heute nachmittag Tennis spielen.
> *The sun is shining. Let's play tennis this afternoon.*

Wo denn?
> *But where?*

Im Klub, wo ich Mitglied bin. Ich reserviere einen Platz.
> *In the club where I am a member. I'll reserve a court.*

Kannst du mir einen Schläger leihen? Ich habe meinen zu
Hause gelassen.
> *Can you lend me a racket? I've left mine at home.*

* * * * * *

Kopf oder Adler[21]?
> *Heads or tail?*

Adler, also schlägst du auf[22].
> *Tail, so its your serve.*

* * * * * *

Fehler!
> *Fault!*

War dieser Ball gut?
> *Was this shot good?*

---

[21] *lit.,* "eagle," shown on German coins.   [22] **aufschlagen, vorschlagen,** §45.

Ja, er traf auf die Linie. — Deine Rückhand ist ja Klasse!
Yes, it hit the line. — Your backhand is really something (lit., is class)!

Das überrascht mich auch, da ich an euren Hartplatz nicht gewöhnt bin. Der Ball springt auf dieser Oberfläche nicht so hoch.
It surprises me, too, since I'm not used to your clay court. The ball doesn't bounce so high on this surface.

Spielen wir zwei oder drei Sätze?
Are we playing two or three sets?

Ich schlage vor[22], daß wir uns nach diesem Satz etwas erfrischen.
I suggest that we have a small refreshment (lit., that we refresh ourselves somewhat) after this set.

Gute Idee.
Good idea.

Im Klub-Restaurant kannst du auch andere Mitglieder kennenlernen.
In the club restaurant you can also get acquainted with other members.

Der Klub gefällt mir. Nur muß ich mir für das nächste Mal ein richtiges Tennishemd kaufen.
I like the club. I'll just have to buy myself a proper tennis shirt for the next time.

Ja, hier spielt man in Weiß gekleidet, ganz, wie es sich gehört.
Yes, here one plays dressed in white, just as it should be (lit., as it is proper).

REMARKS

1. Additional vocabulary: **der Aufschlag,** serve, service; **der Einstand,** deuce; **das Einzel,** single; **das Doppel,** double;

die Grundlinie, base line; **das Netz,** net; **der Netzball,** net ball; **die Partie,** match; **der Punkt,** point; **der Rasenplatz,** lawn court; **der Schiedsrichter,** umpire, referee; **schneiden,** to slice; **das Spiel,** game; **Tennisschuhe,** *m.*, tennis shoes; **die Vorhand,** forehand; **der Vorteil,** advantage; **Wie steht es?** What is the score?

  2. Usage:
gehören, to belong
Der Schläger gehört mir. The racket belongs to me.
sich gehören, to be proper
Es gehört sich nicht, die Spieler zu stören. It is not proper to disturb the players.

Wintersport

Winter Sports

REMARKS

Modern downhill skiing originated in the Alps, of which the **Bundesrepublik** only occupies a small part. The major winter sport areas are in Switzerland, Austria, France, and Italy, roughly in this order of importance. There are areas that permit year-round skiing at altitudes above 8,000 feet and resorts that appeal to every taste and level of skill. In the **Bundesrepublik** there is also some skiing in the mountainous regions of Southern and Central Germany, mainly in the **Schwarzwald** (Black Forest) and the **Harz.**

Schön, daß in St. Moritz[23] so viel los ist!
> *It's great that there is so much going on in St. Moritz!*

Wenn man den ganzen Tag auf der Piste ist, kann man das alles gar nicht ausnützen.
> *If you are on the slopes all day long you can't make use of it all.*

Ich bin Anfängerin und will mir nicht die Knochen brechen.
> *I am a beginner and don't want to break my bones.*

Sie sollten in die Skischule gehen.
> *You should go to the ski school.*

Ja, aber nur vormittags. Der Après-Ski ist schließlich auch wichtig.
> *Yes, but only in the mornings. After all, the après-ski is important, too.*

---

[23] resort in Switzerland.

Ich komme hierher wegen der guten Abfahrten, und weil mir
die Atmosphäre gefällt.

> *I come here because of the good runs and because I like the
> atmosphere.*

Sie sind wohl ein rasanter Skiläufer?

> *You probably are a hot-shot skier?*

Ich kann auf allen Pisten fahren.

> *I can ski on all slopes.*

Wie ich Sie beneide! Ich muß morgen mit dem Schneepflug
anfangen.

> *How I envy you! I have to start with the snow plow to-
> morrow.*

In der zweiten Woche werden Sie schon den Stemmbogen
meistern.

> *By the second week you will already master the stem christie.*

Da bin ich nicht so sicher. Wenn der Abfahrtslauf zu schwie-
rig ist, werde ich Langlauf versuchen.

> *I am not so sure of that. If downhill skiing is too difficult,
> I'll try cross-country skiing.*

Man langweilt sich nie hier, auch wenn man nicht Ski läuft.

> *One is never bored here, even if one doesn't ski.*

Sie haben recht. Man kann spazierengehen, Schlittschuh
laufen, mit dem Pferdeschlitten fahren oder ganz einfach in
der Sonne liegen.

> *You are right. One can take a walk, go skating, take a ride
> in a horse-drawn sleigh, or simply lie in the sun.*

Und wenn man gar nicht aktiv sein will, geht man als
Zuschauer zu einem Eishockeyspiel, Bobrennen oder Ski-
springen.

> *And if one doesn't want to be active at all, one goes as a
> spectator to an ice-hockey game, a bobsled race, or a ski jump.*

Und danach zum Tanz-Tee.
And after that to a tea dance.

REMARKS

1. Additional vocabulary: **der Abfahrtslauf,** downhill race; **die Ausrüstung,** equipment; **die Bindung,** binding; **der Gipfel,** top (of a mountain); **der Gletscher,** glacier; **die Loipe,** cross-country trail; **der Schlepplift,** T-bar; **die Schlittschuhbahn,** skating rink; **die Seilbahn,** cable car; **der Sessellift,** chair lift; **der Ski, der Schi,** ski; **Ski laufen/fahren,** to ski; **das Skilaufen,** skiing; **der Skiläufer,** skier; **der Skilehrer,** ski instructor; **der Skipaß,** ski pass; **der Skistiefel,** ski boot; **der Skistock,** ski pole; **der Skiverleih,** ski rental; **die sportliche, Veranstaltung,** sports event; **die Sprungschanze,** ski jump.

2. Usage:
fahren, to go by; to drive, ride
Ein Auto fahren, to drive a car; **Sie fuhren mit der Eisenbahn.** They went by train.
Schlitten/Ski/Fahrrad/Motorrad/Auto fahren, to ride a sleigh/ to ski/ to ride a bike/motorbike/to drive a car.
Mit dem Bus/dem Zug/der Straßenbahn/der U-Bahn/dem Taxi/dem Schiff fahren (als Passagier), to go by bus/train/ streetcar/subway/Taxi/boat (as a passenger).

Am Strand

On the Beach

REMARKS

The **Bundesrepublik** has a short shoreline on the **Nordsee** (North Sea) and the **Ostsee** (Baltic Sea). The beach season is rather brief, about June to August, and the water never gets very warm. The most famous and fashionable beach resorts are on the island of **Sylt.** Many other islands offer less crowded beaches to people who prefer long walks and observing nature. Most of the sandy Baltic beaches now belong to the GDR. German beaches are dotted with high-backed wicker basket chairs that somewhat resemble baseball gloves in shape. They provide shelter against the prevailing winds.

Wir müssen den Strandkorb etwas drehen.
We have to turn the beach chair somewhat.

Warum denn?
What for?

Ich bin schon teilweise im Schatten.
I am already partially in the shade.

Das habe ich nicht bemerkt.
I didn't notice that.

So ist es besser. Wir haben auch weniger Wind.
That's better. We also have less wind.

Ja, der Wind scheint sich etwas gedreht zu haben.
Yes, the wind seems to have shifted slightly.

Wir sollten morgen eine richtig große Sandburg bauen.
We should build a real big sand castle tomorrow.

Ja, wir werden uns eine Schaufel besorgen.
Yes, we'll get ourselves a shovel.

Komm, laß uns ins Wasser gehen.
Come on, let's go into the water.

Mir ist es zu kalt.
It's too cold for me.

Du kannst dich doch in der Sonne wieder aufwärmen.
But you can warm up again in the sun.

Ich muß mich erst etwas akklimatisieren.
I have to acclimate myself somewhat first.

Na gut. Dann gehe ich jetzt schwimmen.
O.K.   Then I'll go swimming now.

Ich bin dafür[24], daß wir später eine Strandwanderung machen.
I am for taking a walk along the beach later on.

Oh ja, dann werden wir Muscheln sammeln.
Oh yes, then we'll collect shells.

REMARKS

1. Additional vocabulary: **der Badeanzug,** bathing suit; **der Bademantel,** bath robe; **die Bademütze,** bathing cap; **das Badetuch,** beach towel; **braun werden,** to get a tan; **die Düne,** dune; **die Flosse,** fin; **die Kabine,** cabin; **das Meer,** sea; **das Motorboot,** motor boat; **der Ozean,** ocean; **der Schnorchel,** snorkel; **das Segelboot,** sailboat; **der Sonnenbrand,** sunburn; **die Sonnenbrille,** sunglasses; **die (Sonnen)bräune,** suntan; **die Tauchermaske,** diving mask.

[24] §36.

2. Usage:

(etwas) besorgen, to get, to provide (something); to do, to attend to

Ich besorge dir eine Badehose. I'll get bathing trunks for you.

Ich besorge das Kochen. I'll do the cooking.

Proverb: **Was du heute kannst besorgen, das verschiebe nicht auf morgen.** A stitch in time saves nine. (lit., Don't postpone until tomorrow what you can do today.)

Ich bin dafür, daß wir jetzt schwimmen. I am in favor of swimming now.

Ich bin dafür, daß wir nach Hause gehen. I am for going home.

Er ist dafür, daß sie in die Schule geht. He is in favor of her going to school. (lit., He is for it that she should go to school.)

7

Sitten und Bräuche

Customs and Manners

Herr Professor — Gnädige Frau — Ihre Gattin

Professor — Madam — Your Wife

Ich bin morgen bei Professor Müller zum Tee eingeladen. Kannst du mir einige Tips geben?

> *I'm invited for tea at Professor Müller's home tomorrow. Can you give me some pointers?*

Ja, ich glaube, das ist nötig. Müller ist ein guter Professor, sehr nett, aber auch etwas formell. Er muß viel von dir halten, wenn er dich in sein Haus einlädt.

> *Yes, I think that's necessary. Müller is a good professor, very nice, but a bit formal. He must think highly of you if he invites you to his home.*

Soll ich Blumen mitbringen?

> *Should I bring flowers?*

Ja, natürlich.

> *Yes, of course.*

Wie soll ich die Frau von Professor Müller ansprechen?

> *How should I address Professor Müller's wife?*

Sie ist eine ältere Dame. Du sprichst sie mit "Gnädige Frau" an. Du könntest einfach "Frau Müller" sagen, wenn sie in deinem Alter wäre.

> *She is an elderly lady. You address her with "Gnädige Frau." You could simply say "Frau Müller," if she were your age.*

Muß ich sonst noch auf etwas achten?

> *Do I have to pay attention to anything else?*

Ja, sei pünktlich. Komm nicht mehr als zehn Minuten zu spät.

> *Yes, be punctual. Don't be more than ten minutes late.*

Soll ich mich nach dem Besuch schriftlich bedanken?

> *Should I write a thank you note after the visit?*

Nein, das ist nicht nötig. Wenn du Professor Müller in den nächsten Tagen siehst, sagst du zu ihm: "Nochmals vielen Dank für die Einladung, und grüßen Sie Ihre Gattin."

> *No, that is not necessary. When you see Professor Müller on one of the following days, you say to him: "Again many thanks for the invitation and best regards to your wife."*

Warum "Ihre Gattin" und nicht einfach "Ihre Frau"?

> *Why "Ihre Gattin" and not simply "Ihre Frau?"*

Weil du sie nur wenig kennst und weil sie eine "höher gestellte Persönlichkeit" ist.

> *Because you know her only slightly and because she is a person of a certain social rank (lit., a person of higher position).*

Nun hast du mich völlig durcheinandergebracht. Ich weiß nicht, ob ich das schaffen werde.

> *Now you got me all confused. I don't know whether I'll be able to handle the situation.*

Keine Angst, als Ausländer bekommst du "mildernde Umstände".

> *Don't worry, people make allowances (lit., you get mitigating circumstances) since you are a foreigner.*

REMARKS

Although titles are no longer as important in Germany as they used to be, it is still good to know how to properly address the people you have to deal with.

1. Academic titles are part of the name. They can how-ever be used without the name in conversation preceded by **"Herr,"** respectively **"Frau."** Some examples: **Ich möchte Ihnen Herrn Dr. Müller vorstellen.** I'd like to present Dr. Müller to you. **Frau Professor (Meier), Ihre Vorlesung war sehr interessant.** Professor Meier, your lecture was very interesting.

2. Ranks or positions are preceded by **"Herr"** or **"Frau."** Some examples: **Herr Bürgermeister** (mayors of town); **Herr Pfarrer** (Protestant and Catholic clergy); **Herr Minister** (department heads of government); **Herr General** (army general); **Herr Major** (army major); **Frau Direktor** (school principal or company director).

3. Usage:

schriftlich (*adj. and adv.*), written; in writing
mündlich (*adj. and adv.*), verbal, oral
eine schriftliche Prüfung, a written examination; **Du mußt dich schriftlich anmelden.** You have to register in writing.
ein mündliches Abkommen, a verbal agreement; **eine mündliche Prüfung,** an oral examination.

"Sie" oder "du"?

"Sie" or "du"?

Ich habe einen Polizisten gefragt: "Kannst du mir bitte den Weg zur Straßenbahnhaltestelle zeigen?"
I asked a policeman: "Can you please show me the way to the streetcar stop?"

Da hat er sicher ein sehr unfreundliches Gesicht gemacht.
He probably made a very unfriendly face.

Ja, bis ich ihm sagte: "Ich bin Amerikaner."
Yes, till I told him: "I am an American."

Nun, ein Polizist ist aber auch die letzte Person, die man mit "du" anreden würde.
Well, a policeman is really the last person whom one would address with "du."

Wen kann man mit "du" anreden?
Whom can you address with "du?"

Im allgemeinen duzt man nur Familienmitglieder, Kinder, enge Freunde und Haustiere.
In general you address only family members, children, close friends, and pets with "du".

Wirklich? In der Jugendherberge haben alle "du" zu mir gesagt, und ich bin weder ein Kind noch ein Haustier.
Really? In the youth hostel everybody said "du" to me, and I am neither a child nor a pet.

Du hast recht; unter jungen Leuten ist das heute mehr üblich als früher.

> *You are right; that is more customary among young people today than it used to be.*

Die Sache ist also kompliziert?

> *Then it is a complicated matter?*

So ist es. Oft wird das erste "du" bei Leuten "alter Schule" mit einem Glas Wein gefeiert.

> *That is so. People "of the old school" often celebrate the first "du" with a glass of wine.*

Und wenn die Freundschaft aufhört, sagt man dann wieder "Sie"?

> *And when the friendship comes to an end, does one say "Sie" again?*

Das wäre ungewöhnlich. Man redet nicht mehr miteinander oder beschimpft sich[1] per "du".

> *That would be unlikely. People (lit., one) just don't talk to one another any longer or they call each other names saying "du."*

REMARKS

Usage:

duzen = mit "du" anreden; siezen = mit "Sie" anreden.

per, by (means of) (colloq.)

Per is used colloquially in certain combinations: **per Bahn/ per Post/per Eilboten** instead of **mit der Bahn/mit der Post/durch Eilboten,** by train/by mail/by special delivery.

---

[1] reflexives, §47c.

Eine Party

A Party

Schön, euch mal wieder zu sehen. Kommt 'rein[2].
Nice to see you again. Come in.

Wenn du eine Party schmeißt, müssen wir doch dabei sein.
If you throw a party, we sure have to be part of it.

Na klar. — Ihr könnt euere Mäntel hier in der Garderobe aufhängen.
Sure. — You can hang up your coats in the closet.

Sind schon viele da?
Are many here already?

Nein, ihr seid unter den ersten.
No, you are among the first.

Wie viele Leute erwartest du?
How many people are you expecting?

Eingeladen habe ich ungefähr dreißig. Es werden aber meistens mehr.
I've invited about thirty. But usually more come.

Wir haben dir 'ne[3] Flasche mitgebracht — vom Besten.
We've brought you a bottle — one of the best (lit., from the best).

---

[2] colloq. for **herein.**   [3] colloq. for **eine.**

Danke, die können wir gebrauchen. — Ihr kennt doch
Marianne, meine Freundin?
> *Thanks, we can use it. — You know Marianne, my girl
> friend?*

Na klar. Tag,[4] Marianne.
> *Sure. Hi, Marianne.*

Tag, Thomas. Tag, Claudia. Ihr könnt euch selbst bedienen.
Die Getränke sind dort drüben. Das Essen steht auf dem
Tisch.
> *Hi, Thomas. Hi, Claudia. You may help yourselves. The
> drinks are over there. The food is on the table.*

Sag mal, kommen eigentlich Hans und Inge auch?
> *Tell me, are Hans and Inge coming too?*

Nein, die sind mir zu spießig.
> *No, they are too square for me.*

Soll ich 'ne Platte auflegen?
> *Shall I put on a record?*

Ja, tu das mal.
> *Yes, go right ahead (lit., do that).*

Was wollt ihr hören?
> *What do you want to listen to?*

Ich bin für die "Dire Straits".
> *I'm for the "Dire Straits."*

Und ich für die "Bee Gees".
> *And I'm for (lit., I for) the "Bee Gees."*

---

[4] colloq. for **Guten Tag.**

O.K. Einer nach dem andern. — Habt ihr gehört, die "Dire Straits" mußten ihre Norddeutschland-Tournee absagen — wegen Überanstrengung.

> *O.K. One after the other. — Have you heard, the "Dire Straits" had to cancel their tour through Northern Germany — on account of overexertion.*

Ganz schöner Mist[5]. Ich hatte mich schon darauf gefreut.

> *That's too bad. I had already been looking forward to it.*

Ah, es klingelt. Ich geh mal die Tür aufmachen. Vielleicht sind es unsere Freunde aus New York.

> *Ah, the doorbell is ringing. I'll go open the door. Perhaps it's our friends from New York.*

REMARKS

Usage: The following words are sometimes used to add emphasis or to indicate probability, uncertainty, or insistence. In these cases they are often untranslatable or are rendered in English by an entire phrase or by special intonation.

denn:	**Wo ist er denn?** Where is he?
schon:	**Na, beeil dich schon!** Hurry up!
mal:	**Tanzen wir mal?** Let's dance?
ja auch:	**Sie hat es ja auch zugegeben.** After all, she's admitted it.
doch:	**Das ist doch der Zug nach Hamburg?** This is the train to Hamburg, isn't it?
	Er ist es doch gewesen. It was he after all.
wohl:	**Er wird es wohl sein.** It's probably he.
da:	**Da bin ich froh.** I'm glad about it.
nun:	**Wann gibt es nun etwas zu essen?** When do we finally eat?
eben:	**Sie war eben zu alt.** It's because she was too old.

---

[5] frequently-used mild profanity, *lit.* **der Mist** = manure.

eigentlich: **Habt ihr eigentlich ein Auto?** Incidentally, do you have a car?

ja: **Das ist ja sehr praktisch.** That's very practical indeed.

Sometimes several of these words are strung together: **Komm doch mal eben her!** Why don't you come here!

Betreten verboten

No Trespassing

Warum fährst du deinen Wagen immer bis zur nächsten Nebenstraße, wenn du wenden willst? Kannst du nicht die Einfahrt nebenan benützen?

> *Why do you always drive your car to the next side street when you want to turn around? Can't you use the driveway next door?*

Das hat der Nachbar nicht so gern. Hast du nicht das Schild "Betreten verboten" gesehen?

> *The neighbor doesn't like that so much. Haven't you seen the "No Trespassing" sign?*

Ja, das habe ich schon gesehen. Aber du mußt doch nur ein kleines Stück in die Einfahrt fahren.

> *Yes, I did see it. But you have to drive only a little bit into the driveway.*

Die Leute hier nehmen es sehr genau mit der Ordnung. Du hast sicher bemerkt, daß fast jeder Garten mit einem Zaun umgeben ist.

> *People here take order very seriously. You have probably noticed that every garden is surrounded by a fence.*

Ja, alles scheint streng geregelt. Selbst im Stadtpark ist das Betreten des Rasens verboten.

> *Yes, everything seems to be strictly regulated. Even in the City Park stepping on the lawn is forbidden.*

Dafür ist das Gras auch immer grün.

> *That's why the grass is always so green.*

Die Feiertage — Weihnachten

Holidays — Christmas

1. Januar	**Neujahr(stag)**	New Year's Day
6. Januar	**Heilige Drei Könige**	Epiphany
	Ostern	Easter
	(Sonntag und Montag)	
1. Mai	**Tag der Arbeit**	May Day
	Christi Himmelfahrt	Ascension Day
	Pfingsten	Whitsunday
	(Sonntag und Montag)	(Pentecost)
	Fronleichnam	Corpus Christi
17. Juni	**Tag der Deutschen Einheit**	German National Holiday
1. November	**Allerheiligen**	All Saints' Day
22. November	**Buß- und Bettag**	day of prayer and repentance
24. Dezember	**Heiligabend**	Christmas Eve
25./26. Dez.	**Weihnachten**	Christmas[6]
31. Dezember	**Silvester**	New Year's Eve

[6] Germans celebrate Christmas on Christmas Eve **(am Heiligenabend).**

Wie war der Heiligabend bei deinen Verwandten?
How was Christmas Eve at your relatives'?

Sehr beeindruckend. Es ging ziemlich feierlich zu.
Very impressive. It was a rather festive occasion.

Erzähl mir bitte davon. Bei uns war es so prosaisch; alle
kümmerten sich nur um ihre Geschenke.
Tell me about it, please. At our house it was so prosaic;
everybody paid attention only to their gifts.

Gut, ich werde es Dir erzählen: Als die Feier begann, durften
die Kinder in das Weihnachtszimmer. Die Kerzen am
Weihnachtsbaum brannten, und die Geschenke lagen unter
dem Baum.
Okay, I'll tell you. When the celebration started, the children
were allowed into the room where the Christmas tree was
set up. The candles on the Christmas tree were lit, and the
gifts were under the tree.

Waren die Kerzen echte Wachskerzen oder waren es elek-
trische?
Were the candles real wax candles or were they electric ones?

Es waren echte Wachskerzen. Sie dufteten herrlich.
They were real wax candles. They smelled marvelous.

Ich kann mir vorstellen, daß die Freude der Kinder sich
auf die Erwachsenen übertrug.
I can imagine that the children's joy spread to the adults.

Ja, Du hast recht. Alle zusammen sangen Weihnachtslieder.
Yes, you are right. Everybody joined in singing Christmas
carols.

Und die Geschenke?
And the presents?

Die Geschenke wurden nach dem Singen ausgepackt. Die Kinder freuten sich und spielten mit ihren neuen Sachen.

The gifts were opened after the singing. The children enjoyed themselves and played with their new toys.

Was habt ihr gegessen?

What did you eat?

Erst gab es viele Weihnachtsplätzchen und später ein einfaches Abendessen. Die gebratene Gans gab es am 1. Weihnachtsfeiertag.

First we ate (lit., there were) a lot of Christmas cookies and later a simple dinner. The roast goose was served on Christmas Day.

REMARKS

1. Wishing a Merry Christmas: **Fröhliche Weihnachten, Gesegnete Weihnachten, Ein schönes Weihnachtsfest, Schöne Feiertage, Ein frohes Fest.**

2. Wishing a Happy New Year: **Alles Gute zum Neuen Jahr, Viel Glück im Neuen Jahr, Ein glückliches Neues Jahr.**

3. Usage:

Es ging feierlich zu. It was a festive occasion.

Es ging traurig zu. It was a sad occasion.

sich kümmern um, to pay attention to, to take care of, to mind

sich um einen Kranken kümmern, to take care of a sick person;

Er kümmert sich um nichts. He doesn't care about anything.

Sie kümmert sich nur um ihre Kleider. She is interested only in her dresses. **Kümmere dich um deine eigenen Angelegenheiten.** Mind your own business.

Karneval—Fasching—Fastnacht

Carnival —Mardi Gras

Ich war in Köln zum Karneval. Was für eine närrische Zeit! Ich habe selten so viel gelacht, getanzt und gesungen.

> *I was in Cologne for Carnival. What a crazy time! I've rarely laughed, danced, and sung so much.*

Das kann ich mir gut vorstellen. Hast du dich verkleidet?

> *I can very well imagine that. Did you disguise yourself?*

Ja, ich bin als Öl-Scheich gegangen und war übrigens nicht der einzige.

> *Yes, I went as an oil sheik and was not the only one, by the way.*

In Wirklichkeit gibt es ja auch ziemlich viele.

> *In reality there are after all quite a few.*

Da hast du recht. Übrigens habe ich nie in meinem Leben so viele Cowboys und Sheriffs gesehen.

> *You are right. By the way, I have never seen so many cowboys and sheriffs in my life.*

Ja, der "Wilde Westen" ist hier sehr beliebt, auch im Fernsehen.

> *Yes, the "Wild West" is very popular here, also on television.*

Warum gibt es eigentlich so viele verschiedene Namen für den Karneval?

> *Why are there actually so many different names for Carnival?*

Jede Gegend hat ihren eigenen Namen dafür: In Köln ist es der Karneval, in Mainz die Fastnacht oder Fassenacht, in München der Fasching und in der Gegend vom Schwarzwald die Fasnet.

> *Every region has its own name for it: In Cologne it is* Karneval; *in Mainz,* Fastnacht *or* Fassenacht; *in Munich,* Fasching; *and in the Black Forest area,* Fastnet.

Weißt du etwas über den Ursprung des Karnevals?

> *Do you know anything about the origin of Carnival?*

Es gibt wahrscheinlich eine Verbindung zwischen dem Karneval und vorchristlichen Bräuchen beim Wechsel der Jahreszeiten.

> *There is most likely a connection between Carnival and pre-Christian customs at the change of the seasons.*

Der Karneval hat aber auch etwas mit der katholischen Fastenzeit zu tun, nicht wahr?

> *But Carnival also has something to do with the Catholic Lent, doesn't it?*

Ja, der Karneval endet, wenn die Fastenzeit beginnt, am Aschermittwoch.

> *Yes, Carnival ends when Lent begins, on Ash Wednesday.*

REMARKS

Usage:

Was für eine Freude! What a joy! **Was für ein Idiot!** What an idiot!

(jemanden) vorstellen, to introduce, present (somebody)
sich (etwas) vorstellen, to imagine (something)
Darf ich Herrn Miller vorstellen? May I present Mr. Miller to you? **Ich kann mir vorstellen, daß es dir in Deutschland gefallen wird.** I can imagine that you will like it in Germany.

8

Reisen und Besichtigungen

Travels and Sightseeing

Berlin, Gedächtniskirche

Berlin, Memorial Church

REMARKS

From 1871 until 1945 Berlin was the capital of Germany, but for several centuries before that it had been the capital of Prussia. In 1933 Berlin had about 4 million inhabitants. In the war it was heavily bombed, and in 1945 it was conquered by the Soviet army. Since then it has been divided into three Western sectors, i.e., the United States, British, and French, and the Soviet sector, now corresponding to East Berlin. In 1961 the division into East and West Berlin was made complete by the erection of the Berlin Wall.

Guten Tag. Sind Sie Berliner?
Hello. Are you from Berlin?

Ja, ich bin vor fast 70 Jahren hier geboren.
Yes, I was born here almost 70 years ago.

Das trifft sich gut. Darf ich Ihnen ein paar Fragen stellen?
That's great. May I ask you a few questions?

Na klar, junger Mann.
Of course, young man.

Wie war es früher in Berlin?
What was it like in Berlin in the past?

Sie meinen vor der Teilung in Ost- und West-Berlin?
You mean before the division into East and West Berlin?

Ja, und noch früher.
> *Yes, and even before that (lit., and even earlier).*

Früher war Berlin die Hauptstadt von Deutschland und eine richtige Weltstadt.
> *In the past Berlin was the capital of Germany and a real metropolis.*

Sie meinen, das hat mit dem Zweiten Weltkrieg und der Teilung aufgehört.
> *You mean that has ended with the Second World War and the division.*

Ja, heute ist Bonn die Hauptstadt der Bundesrepublik und Ost-Berlin die Hauptstadt der DDR.
> *Yes, today Bonn is the capital of the Federal Republic and East Berlin is the capital of the GDR.*

Es ist aber noch immer[1] viel los hier.
> *But there is still a lot going on here.*

Sicherlich, aber Sie hätten in den Zwanziger Jahren hier sein müssen. Das war die Blütezeit des Theaters und der Kunst in Berlin.
> *Certinly, but you should have been here in the Twenties. That was the heyday of the theater and the arts in Berlin.*

Wie gefällt Ihnen die neue Gedächtniskirche?
> *How do you like the new Memorial Church?*

Der Bau ist sehr nüchtern, aber ich habe mich daran gewöhnt.
> *The building is very austere, but I have gotten used to it.*

Warum hat man die Turmruine neben dem Neubau stehen lassen[2]?
> *Why was the ruin of the tower left standing beside the new building?*

---

[1] **immer,** *always,* here not translatable.   [2] double infinitive, §49f.

Die alte Kirche wurde im Zweiten Weltkrieg durch Bomben zerstört. Man hat die Ruine als Denkmal gegen den[3] Krieg stehen lassen[2].

> *The old church was destroyed by bombs in the Second World War. The ruin was left standing as a memorial against war.*

Waren Sie schon im Innern der Kirche?

> *Have you already been inside the church?*

Ja, natürlich. Sie noch nicht?

> *Yes, of course. You haven't been yet (lit., you not yet)?*

Nein, ich will jetzt hineingehen.

> *No, I want to go in now.*

Ich begleite Sie.

> *I'll accompany you.*

Was für eine Überraschung! Die blauen Glasziegel haben eine fantastische Wirkung.

> *What a surprise! The blue glass bricks have a fantastic effect.*

Man hat das Gefühl, daß man von einem unendlichen blauen Himmel umgeben ist.

> *One has the feeling that one is surrounded by an immense blue sky.*

REMARKS

Usage:

treffen, to hit, to strike
einen Nagel treffen, to hit a nail
(sich) treffen, to meet
Sie trafen ihren Lehrer. They met their teacher.
Sie trafen sich in der Stadt. They met (each other) in town.
Idiomatic use: **Das trifft sich gut.** That's a lucky coincidence. That's great. **Eine Wahl treffen,** to make (hit upon) a choice.

---

[3] use of the article, §2b.

Die Burg des Götz von Berlichingen

Götz von Berlichingen's Castle

Ich möchte gerne eine mittelalterliche Burg sehen, die noch bewohnt ist. Fällt Ihnen dazu etwas ein?

> *I'd like to visit a medieval castle that is still inhabited. Can you think of something?*

Ich glaube, ja. Haben Sie schon vom Götz von Berlichingen gehört, dem "Ritter mit der eisernen Faust"?

> *I believe so. Have you heard about Götz von Berlichingen, the "Knight with the Iron Fist"?*

Ist das nicht ein Stück von Goethe?[4]

> *Isn't that a play by Goethe?*

Richtig. Dieser Ritter hat tatsächlich gelebt, im 16. Jahrhundert. Während der Bauernkriege und der heraufkommenden Reformation kämpfte er für Freiheit und Gerechtigkeit.

> *Right. This knight really lived in the 16th century. During the Peasant Wars and the approaching Reformation he fought for freedom and justice.*

Wo ist die Burg, in der er gewohnt hat?

> *Where is the castle in which he lived?*

Sie liegt in Jagsthausen bei Heilbronn. Die Jagst ist ein Nebenfluß des Neckars.

> *It is located in Jagsthausen near Heilbronn. The Jagst is a river flowing into the Neckar.*

---

[4] German writer, 1749–1832.

Wohnt heute noch jemand in der Burg?
Does anyone still live in the castle today?

Ja, auch heute noch ist der Besitzer ein Ritter mit dem Namen von Berlichingen. Aber lassen Sie mich noch etwas über den Götz und seine Geschichte sprechen.
Yes, even the owner today is a knight by the name of von Berlichingen. But let me talk some more about Götz and his story.

Die Geschichte interessiert mich sehr.
The story interests me very much.

Der Ritter hat den aufregenden Bericht seines Lebens niedergeschrieben in den "Memoiren des Götz von Berlichingen".
The knight recorded the exciting story of his life in the "Memoirs of Götz von Berlichingen."

Hat Goethe die Memoiren gekannt?
Did Goethe know the memoirs?

Ja, Goethe las die Memoiren und nahm sich vor[5], "die Geschichte eines der edelsten Deutschen zu dramatisieren," wie er einem Freund schrieb.
Yes, Goethe read the memoirs and set about "to dramatize the story of one of the most noble Germans," as he wrote to a friend.

Wann war das?
When was that?

Das war um 1780 herum, zur Zeit des Amerikanischen Unabhängigkeitskriegs. Dieses Stück machte den Namen Goethes in ganz Europa bekannt.
It was about 1780, at the time of the American War of Independence. This play made Goethe's name well known throughout Europe.

---

[5] **sich vornehmen,** §45.

Was wissen Sie noch von der Burg?
What else do you know about the castle?

Sie ist seit dem 16. Jahrhundert unverändert. In der Waffen-
kammer kann man die eiserne Faust bewundern, eine vier-
hundert Jahre alte Prothese.
*It has been unchanged since the 16th century. In the armory
one can admire the iron fist, a four-hundred-year-old artificial
limb.*

Die Burg will ich mir unbedingt ansehen, und ich will auch
versuchen, Goethes "Götz" zu lesen.
*I certainly want to have a look at the castle, and I also will
try to read Goethe's "Götz."*

Das wäre eine gute Idee. — Zwischen Anfang Juli und Mitte
August jedes Jahr wird Goethes Schauspiel im Burghof
aufgeführt.
*That would be a good idea. — Between the beginning of
July and the middle of August each year, Goethe's play is
performed in the courtyard of the castle.*

Das ist eine großartige Sache. Dafür muß ich mir unbedingt
Karten besorgen.
That's grand. I must certainly get tickets for it.

Sie sitzen dann im Burghof unter den Zuschauern, und Götz
wird Ihnen allen zurufen: "Kommt setzt euch, tut, als ob
ihr zu Hause wärt, denkt ihr seid wieder einmal beim Götz."
*Then you'll sit in the courtyard of the castle among the
spectators, and Götz will call to you all: "Come, sit down,
act as though you were at home, think that once again you
are at the house of Götz."*

Die Lüneburger Heide

The Luneburg Heath

Ich möchte Ende August eine Radtour machen.
> *I would like to go on a bicycle tour at the end of August.*

Wieviel Zeit wirst du haben?
> *How much time will you have?*

Ungefähr zehn Tage.
> *About ten days.*

Ich kann dir die Lüneburger Heide empfehlen. Sie liegt zwischen Hannover und Hamburg.
> *I can recommend the Luneburg Heath to you. It is located between Hanover and Hamburg.*

Man hat mir gesagt, daß die Heide flach sei[6]. Ich will mich nicht zu sehr anstrengen.
> *I've been told that the heath is flat. I don't want to exert myself too much.*

Ja, sie ist ideal zum Radfahren. Das Heidekraut blüht im Spätsommer. Es ist wunderschön, wie ein violetter Teppich.
> *Yes, it is ideal for bicycling. The heather is in bloom in late summer. It is beautiful, like a violet carpet.*

Ich habe schon Fotos von der Landschaft gesehen. Sie gefällt mir sehr.
> *I've already seen photos of the countryside. I like it very much.*

---

[6] subjunctive in indirect speech, §56.

Sie ist noch wirklich unverdorben. Große Nadel- und Laub-wälder wechseln ab[7] mit der typischen Heidelandschaft.

> *It's still really unspoiled. Large coniferous and deciduous forests alternate with the typical heath landscape.*

Ich möchte auch etwas reiten, wenn möglich.

> *I would also like to do some horseback riding, if possible.*

Man kann praktisch überall Pferde mieten. Es gibt auch viele öffentliche Schwimmbäder und schöne Flüsse zum Bootfahren und Angeln.

> *One can rent horses practically everywhere. There are also many public swimming pools and beautiful rivers for boating and fishing.*

Das klingt verlockend. Du hast mich überzeugt.

> *That sounds tempting. You have convinced me.*

---

[7] **abwechseln,** §45.

Ein Wochenende in München

A Weekend in Munich

Grüß dich, Rosmarie. Endlich bin ich mal[8] wieder in München.
> *Greetings, Rosmarie. Finally I am in Munich once again.*

Grüß dich, Astrid. Das wurde auch höchste Zeit! Immerhin ist es zehn Jahre her, daß du hier gelebt hast.
> *Greetings, Astrid. It's high time! After all, it's ten years since you've lived here.*

Wie schnell die Zeit vergeht! So lange kommt es mir gar nicht vor.
> *How fast time passes. It doesn't seem that long to me at all.*

Du wirst sehen, **München hat sich verändert.**
> *You'll see, Munich has changed.*

Na ja, die U-Bahn wurde gebaut und das Olympiagelände. Ich hoffe, München ist die "Weltstadt mit Herz" geblieben.
> *Well, the subway has been built and the Olympic grounds. I hope Munich has remained the "Metropolis with a Heart."*

Aber natürlich. — Die Fußgängerzone hat die Atmosphäre in der Innenstadt sehr verändert.
> *But of course. — The pedestrian zone has very much changed the atmosphere in the inner city.*

---

[8] **mal** = **einmal.**

Ich bin neugierig, das zu sehen. Sicher ist es gemütlicher geworden.

> *I am curious to see that. It probably has become more leisurely.*

Zwischen Stachus[9] und Marienplatz[9] war früher ein Verkehrschaos; von gemütlich konnte damals keine Rede sein.

> *Between Stachus and Marienplatz there used to be a traffic chaos; one couldn't call that leisurely at the time.*

Ich möchte heute gleich einen Stadtbummel[10] im Zentrum machen und vorher vielleicht Weißwürste[11] essen und ein Bier trinken.

> *Today I'd like to take a stroll through the center of town and before that perhaps eat "Weißwürste" and have a beer.*

Gut, gehen wir in den Ratskeller[12]. — Für heute abend hab'[13] ich Karten für's[14] Nationaltheater besorgt. Das Bolschoi-Ballett ist hier zu den Ballettfestwochen.

> *Fine, we'll go to the Ratskeller. — For this evening I've got tickets for the Nationaltheater. The Bolshoi Ballet is here for the Ballet Festival.*

Großartig! — Morgen früh würde ich gerne an den Tegernsee[15] fahren zum Baden.

> *Great! — Tomorrow morning I'd like to go to the Tegernsee to go swimming (lit., bathing).*

Ja, wir nehmen den Zug. Das ist am einfachsten.

> *Yes, we'll take the train. That's the easiest.*

Und abends kommen wir rechtzeitig zurück, um einen Bummel durch Schwabing[16] zu machen.

> *And in the evening we'll get back in time to take a stroll through Schwabing.*

---

[9] well-known squares in Munich. [10] **der Bummel** = stroll. [11] sausages, a Munich specialty. [12] popular restaurant. [13] **hab'** = **habe**. [14] **für's** = **für das.** [15] scenic lake near Munich. [16] district where many artists and students live and there is much night life.

Gute Idee. Heute ist das Wetter schön. Man kann im Freien sitzen.

> *Good idea. Today the weather is nice. One can sit outside.*

Stellen die Künstler ihre Sachen immer noch auf der Leopoldstraße[17] aus?

> *Do the artists still show their works (lit., things) on Leopoldstraße?*

Na klar. — Du solltest dir aber auch die Nolde[18]-Ausstellung im Haus der Kunst[19] ansehen.

> *Sure enough. — You should also take a look at the Nolde exhibition in the Haus der Kunst (House of Art).*

Das kann ich Montag früh tun. Mein Zug fährt erst um halb zwei.

> *I can do that Monday morning. My train doesn't leave until 1:30 P.M.*

REMARKS

Usage:

kommen, to come
vorkommen, to occur, happen
Früher kamen wilde Pferde in Europa vor. In former times there were wild horses in Europe. **Es kann vorkommen, daß man sich irrt.** It can happen that one makes a mistake. **Es kommt mir/dir/ihm/ihr/uns/euch/ihnen/Ihnen vor . . .** It seems to me/you/him/her/us/you/them/you . . . **Es kommt mir vor, als ob es klingelt.** It seems to me as if the bell rings.
Proverb: **Das kommt mir spanisch vor.** That seems fishy to me. (lit., It seems Spanish to me.)

Wir machen einen Spaziergang. We take a walk.
Wir machen ein Foto. We take a photo.
Wir machen Ferien. We take a vacation.
Wir machen eine Reise. We take a trip.

---

[17] main street in Schwabing.   [18] Emil Nolde, 1867–1956, modern German painter.
[19] modern art museum.

In spoken German one can tell quarter hours by counting the fraction of the ongoing hour prior to the full hour:

halb zwei = **1.30 Uhr,** half past one (lit., half two)

Viertel fünf = **Viertel nach vier** = **4.15 Uhr,** a quarter past four

drei Viertel sechs = **Viertel vor sechs** = **17.45 Uhr,** a quarter to six.

drei Viertel zwölf = **Viertel vor zwölf** = **11.45 Uhr,** a quarter to twelve.

Salzburg

Salzburg

"Salzburg[20] hat sein Gesicht bewahrt." So heißt es in einem Prospekt über die Stadt.
> *"Salzburg has kept its character (lit., face)." This is what it says in a brochure about the town.*

Was meint man damit?
> *What is meant by that?*

Man meint, daß die Altstadt noch genauso aussieht wie[21] zur Zeit Mozarts[22].
> *It means that the old city still looks as it did at the time of Mozart.*

Mozarts Geburtshaus habe ich gestern besucht. Er wurde 1756 hier geboren.
> *Yesterday I visited the house where Mozart was born. He was born here in 1756.*

Salzburg ist eine Stadt mit einer langen Geschichte: Kelten, Römer und Germanen haben hier schon gesiedelt. Der Name kommt von dem Salz, das seit der Antique in der Gegend gefördert wird.
> *Salzburg is a town with a long history: Celts, Romans, and Germanic tribes settled here. The name comes from the salt that has been mined in the area since antiquity.*

---

[20] historical Austrian town close to the German border.   [21] comparison of equality, §23.   [22] Austrian composer.

Ich finde die Lage an der Salzach zwischen den Hügeln so besonders schön.

> *I find the location in the hills on the Salzach River particularly beautiful.*

Ich bin ganz deiner Meinung. Die barocke Altstadt mit dem Dom und die Festung auf einem der Hügel gehören zu dieser Landschaft.

> *I fully share your opinion. The baroque old city with the cathedral and the fortress on one of the hills belong to this landscape.*

Man merkt, daß die Stadt seit Jahrhunderten Sitz der Erzbischöfe von Salzburg ist.

> *One is aware that the town has been the see of the archbishops of Salzburg for centuries.*

Sie ließen den Dom, die Festung, viele Kirchen, Residenzen, Gärten und Brunnen erbauen.

> *They had the cathedral, the fortress, many churches, residences, gardens, and fountains built.*

Zur Zeit der Festspiele wird die ganze Stadt zur Bühne.

> *At the time of the festival the whole town becomes a stage.*

Das kann man wohl sagen. "Jedermann"[23], das Spiel vom Sterben des reichen Mannes, wird auf dem Domplatz aufgeführt.

> *You can say that again. "Everyman," the play about the rich man's death, is performed on the Cathedral square.*

Das Schloß Hellbrunn mit seinem Park wird zum Schauplatz vieler Aufführungen. Und es gibt richtiges Straßentheater auf den alten Höfen und Plätzen der Stadt.

> *Hellbrunn Castle with its park becomes the scene of many performances. And there is real street theater in the old courtyards and squares of the town.*

---

[23] play by Hugo von Hofmannsthal, Austrian dramatist, 1874–1929.

Dazu kommen die Festspielhäuser, das Landestheater, das Mozarteum[24] und die Kirche St. Peter, wo Opern, Theaterstücke, Liederabende und Konzerte gegeben werden.

> *In addition there are the festival buildings, the State Theater, the Mozarteum, and St. Peter's Church, where operas, plays, song recitals (lit., song evenings) and concerts are presented.*

Die Festspiele sind zu einem gesellschaftlichen Ereignis geworden. Eintrittskarten bekommt man nur bei rechtzeitiger Vorbestellung.

> *The festival has become a social event. One can get tickets only by ordering them well in advance.*

Aber auch ohne die Festspiele ist Salzburg eine Reise wert.

> *But even without the festival Salzburg is worth a visit (lit., trip).*

REMARKS

Usage:

(etwas) (be)merken, to notice (something)

Er merkte, daß jemand im Zimmer war. He noticed that someone was in the room.

sich (etwas) merken, to memorize (something), to commit (something) to one's memory

Er merkte sich die Hausnummer. He memorized the house number.

The verbs **werden** and **bekommen** are frequently confused, since both can mean "get."

werden, to become, get; **bekommen,** to receive, get

Der Schauspieler wurde krank. The actor got (became) sick.

Das Schloß wird zum Schauplatz vieler Aufführungen. The castle becomes the scene of many performances.

Ich habe zwei Karten bekommen. I got (received) two tickets.

---

[24] music school.

Eine Reise in der Vergangenheit

A Journey in the Past

Wie die Leute im Mittelalter gereist sind, wissen wir zum Beispiel aus dem Reisetagebuch Dürers[25].

We know how people traveled in the Middle Ages from Dürer's travel diary, for example.

Dürer lebte um 1500 in Nürnberg, nicht wahr? Hast du sein Tagebuch gelesen?

Dürer lived in Nürnberg around 1500, didn't he? Have you read his diary?

Ja, Auszüge daraus. Es ist hauptsächlich ein Bericht über Ausgaben, Einkäufe und Geschenke.

Yes, excerpts from it. It is mainly an account of expenditures, purchases, and gifts.

Welche Reisen hat er unternommen?

Which travels did he undertake?

1520 war er zweimal in Köln.

In 1520 he was in Cologne twice.

Wie ist er nach Köln gereist?

How did he travel to Cologne?

Er ist auf dem Main und dem Rhein mit dem Schiff gefahren.

He went by boat on the Main and the Rhine rivers.

Wie lange ist er unterwegs gewesen?

How long was he on his way?

[25] German painter, 1471–1528.

Zwei Wochen. Er kam bei der ersten Reise am 25. Juli in Köln an[26]. Zwischen Bamberg und Köln mußte er 32 Zollkontrollen passieren.

> *Two weeks. On the first trip he arrived in Cologne on July 25. Between Bamberg and Cologne he had to pass 32 custom checkpoints.*

Das kann nicht wahr sein! Mußte er überall Zoll bezahlen?

> *That can't be true! Did he have to pay duty everywhere?*

Nein, er hatte einen Zollbrief seines Herren, des Bischofs von Bamberg, der von den meisten Kontrollen anerkannt wurde.

> *No, he had a customs pass (lit., letter) from his sovereign, the Bishop of Bamberg, which was recognized by most controls.*

Da hat er ja Glück gehabt. — Ist er allein gereist?

> *He was lucky there. — Did he travel alone?*

Er wurde von seiner Frau Agnes und einer Magd begleitet.

> *He was accompanied by his wife Agnes and a maid.*

Was hat Dürer über Köln berichtet?

> *What did Dürer report about Cologne?*

Köln war damals eine der schönsten Städte Europas. Aber er hat nichts davon erwähnt. Er hat uns auch keine Zeichnung hinterlassen.

> *Cologne was one of the most beautiful cities in Europe at the time. But he didn't mention anything about it. Nor has he left behind a sketch.*

Schade, daß es noch keine Kameras gab.

> *What a shame that there were no cameras yet.*

Wir wissen aber, wie Köln damals aussah. Es gibt sehr schöne Stiche von anderen Künstlern.

> *But we know what Cologne looked like at the time. There are very beautiful engravings by other artists.*

---

[26] **ankommen**, §45.

Den Dom hat es sicher schon gegeben.
The Cathedral probably existed already.

Es gab den Dom, viele Kirchen und schöne Bürgerhäuser, umgeben von einer Stadtmauer.
There was the Cathedral, many churches, and private homes (lit., houses of burghers) surrounded by a city wall.

Was war eigentlich der Zweck von Dürers Reise?
What was actually the purpose of Dürer's journey?

Auf seiner ersten Reise war Köln nur eine Zwischenstation auf dem Weg nach Antwerpen.
On his first journey, Cologne was only a stop on the way to Antwerp.

Wann ist Dürer das zweite Mal in Köln gewesen?
When was Dürer in Cologne the second time?

Er kam am 28. Oktober in Köln an[26]. Die Kaiserkrönung Karls V.[27] hatte am 23. Oktober in Aachen stattgefunden.
He arrived in Cologne on October 28. The coronation of Emperor Charles V had taken place in Aachen on October 23.

Sie war sicher das politische Ereignis des Jahres. — Hat Dürer darüber in seinem Tagebuch berichtet?
It was probably the political event of the year. — Did Dürer tell about it in his diary?

Ja, der Kaiser kam am 30. Oktober nach Köln, und Dürer hat an den Festlichkeiten in der Stadt teilgenommen.
Yes, the emperor arrived in Cologne on October 30, and Dürer took part in the festivities in the town.

---

[27] King of Spain and Emperor of the Holy Roman Empire, which included Germany and Austria.

9
Korrespondenz

Correspondence

Redewendungen

Phrases

■ **Anreden**   *Forms of address*

Sehr geehrter Herr Thomas,	*Dear Mr. Thomas:* (formal)
Sehr geehrte Herren,	*Gentlemen:* (in business letters)
Sehr geehrter Herr Dr. Müller,	*Dear Dr. Müller:*
Sehr geehrter Herr Professor,	*Dear Professor:*
Lieber Herr Meier,	*Dear Mr. Meier:*
Lieber Peter,	*Dear Peter:*
Sehr geehrte Frau Thomas,	*Dear Mrs. Thomas:* (formal)
Sehr geehrte Frau Dr. Müller,	*Dear Dr. Müller:* (lady doctor)
Sehr geehrte Frau Professor,	*Dear Professor:* (lady professor)
Liebe Frau Meier,	*Dear Mrs. Meier:*
Liebe Anne,	*Dear Anne:*

■ **Briefschluß**   *Letter closings*

Hochachtungsvoll	*Yours very truly,* (formal)
Mit freundlichen Grüßen	*Sincerely yours,* (current usage in business letters)
Mit besten Grüßen	*Kind regards,* (rather formal, in
Ihr Karl Meier	social correspondence)
	Karl Meier
Mit herzlichem Gruß	*Cordially yours,* (acquaintances)
Ihr Karl Meier	*Karl Meier*
Viele liebe Grüße	*Love,* (relatives and close
Deine Dagmar	friends)
	Dagmar

Geschäftsbriefe

Business Letters

■ **Bestellung**   *An order*

Emil Schütze
Import–Export
z.Hd. Herrn Klaus Wirth
Linden Allee 68
2000 Hamburg

2. Mai 19–

Sehr geehrter Herr Wirth,

liefern Sie mir bitte so schnell wie möglich die folgenden Artikel: . . .

Da ich die Ware dringend benötige, bitte ich um sofortige Auftragsbestätigung mit Liefertermin.

Falls die Lieferung noch vor dem 15. Mai erfolgt, bitte ich um
Versand per Frachtgut; nach diesem Termin per Expreß.

Mit freundlichen Grüßen

Otto Müller

* * * * * *

Emil Schütze
Import–Export
Att. Mr. Klaus Wirth
Linden Allee 68
2000 Hamburg

May 2, 19–

Dear Mr. Wirth:

Please send me the following articles as soon as possible: . . .

Since I urgently require the merchandise, I kindly ask you for immediate confirmation of the order, including delivery date.

If delivery will take place before May 15, I would like to request shipment by normal freight; after this date by express.

Sincerely yours,

Otto Müller

■ **Auftragsbestätigung**   *Confirmation of order*

6. Mai 19–

Sehr geehrter Herr Müller,

wir danken Ihnen für Ihre Bestellung vom 2. Mai und teilen Ihnen mit, daß die Lieferung Ihrer Waren am 10. Mai per Frachtgut erfolgt.

Leider sind wir gezwungen, unsere Preise ab 1. Juni etwas zu erhöhen. Unsere neuen Preise entnehmen Sie bitte der beigefügten Preisliste.

Mit freundlichen Grüßen

Anlage   Klaus Wirth

May 6, 19–

Dear Mr. Müller:

We thank you for your order of May 2 and would like to inform you that the shipment of your merchandise will take place on May 10 by normal freight.

Unfortunately we are forced to increase our prices slightly starting (lit., from) June 1. You will find our new prices (lit., please take our new prices from) in the enclosed price list.

Sincerely Yours,

Encl.   Klaus Wirth

Privatbriefe

Personal Letters

- **Ein Brief an eine Freundin**   *A letter to a friend*

Frankfurt, den 12. Juni

Liebe Judy,

ich freue mich sehr, daß Du jetzt in Deutschland bist und eine gute Reise gehabt hast. Du hast sicherlich schon viele Pläne gemacht und willst Land und Leute kennenlernen.

Ich möchte Dich auf alle Fälle sehen und Dich zu uns nach Frankfurt einladen. Frankfurt ist eine interessante Stadt. Ich habe Zeit und kann Dir vieles zeigen. Du kannst gerne bei uns wohnen.

Laß mich bald wissen, ob Dir mein Vorschlag gefällt.

Alles Liebe

Deine Ruth

* * * * * *

Frankfurt, June 12

Dear Judy:

I am glad that you are now in Germany and have had a good journey. Probably you've made a lot of plans and would like to get to know people and places (lit., country and people).

In any case I'd like to see you and invite you to our place in Frankfurt. Frankfurt is an interesting city. I have time and can show you a lot. You can stay with us.

Let me know soon if you like my suggestion.

Love,

Ruth

■ **Antwort auf den vorangegangen Brief**   *Reply to the preceding letter*

München, den 16. Juni

Liebe Ruth,

Dein Brief hat mich sehr gefreut. Du hast ganz recht: ich will möglichst viel von Deutschland sehen und auch möglichst viele Leute kennenlernen.

Natürlich komme ich gern zu Euch nach Frankfurt und nehme dankend Deine Einladung an. Ich könnte Anfang Juli kommen und etwa eine Woche bleiben. Laß mich wissen, ob Dir diese Zeit paßt.

Bis auf bald.

Alles Liebe

Deine Judy

* * * * * *

Munich, June 16

Dear Ruth,

I enjoyed your letter very much. You are quite right: I'd like to see as much of Germany as possible and also get to know as many people as possible.

Of course I'll gladly come to see you (lit., come to you) in Frankfurt and I accept your invitation with thanks. I could come early in July and stay about one week. Let me know if this time is convenient for you.

Until soon.

Love,

Judy

Glückwünsche

Congratulations

■ Geburtstag   *Birthday*

Liebe Mutter,

zu Deinem Geburtstag möchte ich Dir die allerbesten Glück-
wünsche senden. Ich denke an Dich. Mach Dir einen schönen
Tag. Ein Päckchen ist bereits an Dich unterwegs.

Dein Hannes

Dear Mother:

On your birthday I would like to send you my best wishes. I am
thinking of you. Have a nice day. A package is already on the way
to you.

Hannes

■ Weihnachten und Neujahr   *Christmas and New Year*

Zum Weihnachtsfest und für das Neue Jahr senden wir Euch die
besten Wünsche.

Vera und Peter

Wir wünschen Euch ein fröhliches Weihnachten und ein glückliches Neues Jahr.

Eure Beate und Euer Peter
mit Kindern

Wir senden Ihnen die besten Wünschen für die Feiertage.

Familie **Meier**

* * * * * *

We are sending you best wishes for Christmas and the New Year.

Vera and Peter

With best wishes for a Merry Christmas and a Happy New Year.

Beate and Peter
with children

We are sending you the Season's Greetings.

Family Meier

Wichtige Adressen

Important Addresses

■ **Reisen**   *Travel*

German National Tourist Office
630 Fifth Avenue
New York, N.Y. 10020
Tel. (212) 757-8570/71/72

German Federal Railroad
630 Fifth Avenue
New York, N.Y. 10020
Tel. (212) 977-9300

Deutsche Zentrale für Tourismus (Tourist Information)
Beethovenstraße 69
6900 Frankfurt am Main
Tel. 0611/75721

Deutscher Fremdenverkehrsverband (Tourist Information)
Untermainanlage 6
6000 Frankfurt am Main 1
Tel. 0611/236351

Allgemeine Deutsche Zimmerreservierung (ADZ) (Hotel Reserva-
    tion)
Beethovenstraße 61
6000 Frankfurt am Main 1
Tel. 0611/740767

Deutscher Camping-Club (DCC)
Mandlstraße 28
8000 München 40
Tel. 089/334021

Deutsches Jugendherbergswerk (Youth Hostels)
Bülowstraße 26
4930 Detmold
Tel. 05231/22771-72

Allgemeiner Deutscher Automobil-Club (ADAC)
Baumgartnerstraße 53
8000 München 70
Tel. 089/7676-1

■ **Studentenaustausch**   *Student Exchange*

Deutscher Akademischer Austauschdienst (DAAD)
Kennedyallee 50
5300 Bonn-Bad Godesberg
Tel. 02221/8821

Organisation für Internationale Kontakte
Rheinallee 68
5300 Bonn-Bad Godesberg
Tel. 02221/357015

Goethe-Institut
Lenbachplatz 3
8000 München
Tel. 089/59991

APPENDIX

1. The Definite Article *the*

| | SINGULAR | | | PLURAL | |
	Masc.	*Fem.*	*Neuter*	*All Genders*	
Nom.	**der**	**die**	**das**	**die**	(the)
Gen.	**des**	**der**	**des**	**der**	(of the)
Dat.	**dem**	**der**	**dem**	**den**	(to the)
Acc.	**den**	**die**	**das**	**die**	(the)

2. The definite article is used:

   a. With the seasons, months, and days of the week:
   Der Sommer ist da. Summer is here.
   Der Mai ist schön. May is nice.
   Der Sonntag ist zu kurz. Sunday is too short.

   b. With nouns in general statements:
   Das Leben ist schön. Life is beautiful.

   c. With feminine names of countries:
   die Schweiz Switzerland **die Türkei** Turkey

   d. Instead of the possessive adjective with parts of the body and articles of clothing when the meaning is clear:
   Er zieht sich den Mantel aus. He is taking off his overcoat.

223

Was haben Sie in der Hand.   What do you have in your hand?

Er setzt sich den Hut auf.   He puts on his hat.

e. With nouns of weight and measure:

Es kostet einen Dollar das Pfund.   It costs a dollar a pound.

Er bezahlt zwei Dollar für den Meter.   He pays two dollars a meter.

f. With all place and street names:

Ich bin in der Schule.   I am in school.

Er geht in die Kirche.   He goes to church.

Sie wohnt in der Königsstraße.   She lives on King Street.

g. After prepositions:

Nach dem Frühstück arbeiten wir.   After breakfast we work.

Vor dem Abendessen liest er.   Before supper he reads.

h. With infinitives used as nouns (all are neuter):

Das Arbeiten ist notwendig.   Working (to work) is necessary.

3. The Indefinite Article *a, an*

| | SINGULAR | | | PLURAL (lacking, but may be provided by **manche** or **einige,** *some*) | |
	Masc.	*Fem.*	*Neuter*		
N.	**ein**	**eine**	**ein**	a	**einige** some
G.	**eines**	**einer**	**eines**	of a	**einiger** of some
D.	**einem**	**einer**	**einem**	to a	**einigen** to some
A.	**einen**	**eine**	**ein**	a	**einige** some

4. The indefinite article (**ein, eine**) is omitted:

a. Before unmodified predicate nouns denoting rank, vocation, or station in life

Ich bin Student. I am a student.
Er ist Amerikaner. He is an American.
BUT: **Er ist ein guter Arzt.** He is a good doctor.

b. Before **hundert,** *a hundred,* and **tausend,** *a thousand,* when modifying a noun:

Da waren hundert Leute. There were a hundred people.

5. In **was für ein, was für eine,** *what kind of, what a,* **manch ein, manch eine,** *many a,* and **solch ein, solch eine,** *such a,* only the indefinite article is declined. The indefinite article does not appear with the corresponding plural forms: **was für, manche, solche.**

Was für ein Buch ist das? What kind (type) of a book is this?
Was für Bücher lesen Sie? What type of books do you read?

6. Gender of Nouns

Nouns are masculine, feminine, or neuter. The gender of nouns must be learned with the word itself because the rules concerning gender do not cover all cases. Here are some rules without exceptions.

a. If a noun denotes a male being, it is masculine; if it denotes a female being, it is feminine:

der Mann	the man	**die Frau**	the woman
der Vater	the father	**die Mutter**	the mother

b. Masculine: the four seasons, the months, the days of the week, the points of the compass:

der Herbst	autumn	**der Sonntag**	Sunday
der Januar	January	**der Osten**	east

c. Feminine: most names of trees:

die Birke birch   **die Eiche** oak   **die Pappel** poplar

d. Neuter: cities, letters, fractions, and young animals or children

das alte Heidelberg   old Heidelberg
das große A capital A   **das Kind**   the child
das Fünftel the fifth   **das Füllen** the filly

7. Nouns ending

a. in **-e, -ie, -ei, -heit, -keit, -kunft, -in, -schaft, -ung, -ion,** and **-tät** are feminine:

die Freiheit liberty   **die Zukunft**   the future

b. in **-chen, -lein, -nis, -sal,** and **-tum** are neuter:

das Fräulein the young lady   **das Schicksal** the fate

c. in **-er, -el, -ling** are generally masculine:

der Gärtner the gardner   **der Schlüssel** the key

8. Plural of Nouns

The plural forms of German nouns sometimes have an umlaut (¨) and no additional ending, *or* they add an **-e** *or* **-er** and umlaut, *or* they add **-(e)n** without an umlaut. Accordingly, the majority of German nouns may be divided into four plural classes:

a. Most masculine nouns ending in **-el, -er,** or **-en** and all neuter nouns ending in **-chen** or **-lein** (diminutives) have no plural endings and may or may not have umlauts:

der Vater   **die Väter**   the fathers
der Kuchen **die Kuchen** the cakes

There are only two feminine nouns in this class:

die Mutter   **die Mütter**   mothers
die Tochter **die Töchter** daughters

b. Most monosyllabic masculine nouns and some feminine and neuter nouns add an **-e** and sometimes an umlaut:

der Baum	**die Bäume**	trees
das Jahr	**die Jahre**	years
die Hand	**die Hände**	hands
der Brief	**die Briefe**	letters

c. Most monosyllabic neuter nouns and some masculine nouns (but no feminine nouns) add an **-er** and an umlaut:

das Haus	**die Häuser**	houses
der Mann	**die Männer**	men
das Kind	**die Kinder**	children
das Kleid	**die Kleider**	dresses

d. Most feminine nouns and some masculine and neuter nouns add an **-(e)n ;** they never have an umlaut:

die Frau	**die Frauen**	women
die Gabel	**die Gabeln**	forks
der Herr	**die Herren**	gentlemen
das Ohr	**die Ohren**	ears

9. The only general rule for the plural of nouns is that all dative plurals must end in **-n :**

N.	**die Männer**	**die Frauen**	**die Kinder**
	(the men)	(the women)	(the children)
G.	**der Männer**	**der Frauen**	**der Kinder**
D.	**den Männern**	**den Frauen**	**den Kindern**
A.	**die Männer**	**die Frauen**	**die Kinder**

10. Singular of Nouns

Masculine and neuter nouns generally add an **-(e)s** in the genitive singular; feminine nouns never add an ending in the singular:

N.	**der Mann**	**die Frau**	**das Kind**
	(the man)	(the woman)	(the child)
G.	**des Mannes**	**der Frau**	**des Kindes**

D. **dem Mann**   **der Frau**   **dem Kind**
A. **den Mann**   **die Frau**   **das Kind**

11. Those masculine nouns that form the plural in **-(e)n** have an **-(e)n** in all singular cases except the nominative:

    N. **der Mensch**   **der Herr**
       (the human being)   (the gentleman)
    G. **des Menschen**   **des Herrn**
    D. **dem Menschen**   **dem Herrn**
    A. **den Menschen**   **den Herrn**

12. Principal Parts of Nouns

The only sure way to learn the declension of a German noun is to know the nominative singular, the genitive singular, and the nominative plural forms. These are the principal parts of the noun:

    der Name (the name), **des Namens, die Namen**
    der Bruder (the brother), **des Bruders, die Brüder**

In abbreviated form:

    der Name, -ns, -n name
    der Bruder, -s, ¨-, brother

13. Use of the Cases

German has four cases: nominative, genitive, dative, and accusative. The nominative is used as subject and predicate noun and in address:

    Der Mann arbeitet. The man works.
    Er ist Lehrer. He is a teacher.
    Guten Tag, Herr Braun. Good morning, Mr. Brown.

The genitive denotes possession. Note that in German the apostrophe is not used to indicate the possessive:

    der Hut des Mannes the man's hat
    Karls Buch Karl's book
    Emils Freund Emil's friend

The dative is the case of the indirect object:

> **Geben Sie dem Mann das Geld.**   Give the money to the man.

The accusative is the case of the direct object:

> **Ich habe einen Freund.**   I have a friend.

14. Prepositions

Aside from the fundamental meaning of cases, the genitive, dative, and accusative forms must be used after certain prepositions. These are:

a. for the genitive:

(an)statt	instead of	**während**	during
trotz	in spite of	**wegen**	on account of
um...willen	for the sake of		

> **Wir arbeiten während des Tages.**   We work during the day.

b. for the dative:

aus	out of, from	**nach**	after, to
außer	besides	**seit**	since
bei	at, near	**von**	from, of
mit	with	**zu**	to

> **Er schreibt mit dem Bleistift.**   He writes with the pencil.

NOTE: **von** + dative often replaces a genitive:

> **der Bruder von Andrea = Andreas Bruder**   Andrea's brother
> **der Mann von ihr = ihr Mann**   her husband

c. for the accusative:

durch	through	**gegen**	against	**um**	around
für	for	**ohne**	without		

> **Er bezahlt für seinen Freund.**   He pays for his friend.

d. for the dative or accusative:

an	at, to	**über**	over, above
auf	on, upon	**unter**	under, beneath
hinter	behind	**vor**	before, in front of
in	in, into	**zwischen**	between
neben	next to		

These words govern the dative when the question is: "Where does it take place?" or "Where is it?"

Wo ist das Buch? — Auf dem Tisch.   Where is the book? — On the table.

Wo arbeitet er? — In seinem Zimmer.   Where does he work? — In his room.

They are followed by the accusative when the verb expresses a motion toward a place:

Wohin gehen Sie? — In die Stadt.   Where are you going? — Into the city.

Er stellt das Glas auf den Tisch.   He puts the glass on the table.

15. Contractions of prepositions with the definite article:

an dem = am	at the
an das = ans	to the
auf das = aufs	on the
bei dem = beim	at the
durch das = durchs	through the
um das = ums	around the
für das = fürs	for the
in dem = im	in the
in das = ins	in the
von dem = vom	from the
zu dem = zum	to the
zu der = zur	to the

16. Adjectives

a. Predicate adjectives remain unchanged:

Das Buch ist gut.   The book is good.

Die Bücher sind gut.   The books are good.

b. Adjectives that follow definite articles, demonstratives, or interrogatives have an **-en** ending in all case forms, except the nominative singular of all three genders and the accusative singular of the feminine and neuter, which end in **-e**:

SINGULAR

Masc.	*Neuter*	*Fem.*
N. **der gute Freund**	**das neue Buch**	**die gute Frau**
G. **des guten Freundes**	**des neuen Buches**	**der guten Frau**
D. **dem guten Freund**	**dem neuen Buch**	**der guten Frau**
A. **den guten Freund**	**das neue Buch**	**die gute Frau**

PLURAL

M. F. N.

N. **die neuen Bücher**
G. **der neuen Bücher**
D. **den neuen Büchern**
A. **die neuen Bücher**

c. Adjectives that follow indefinite articles, the negative **kein(e)**, or the possessives (**mein, dein, sein,** etc.) also have an **-en** ending in all cases, except the nominative singular of all genders, where they end in **-er, -es,** or **-e** according to gender, and the accusative singular of the neuter (**-es**) and feminine (**-e**):

SINGULAR

Masc.	*Neuter*
N. **ein guter Mann**	**kein neues Buch**
G. **eines guten Mannes**	**keines neuen Buches**
D. **einem guten Mann**	**keinem neuen Buch**
A. **einen guten Mann**	**kein neues Buch**

Fem.

eine gute Frau
einer guten Frau
einer guten Frau
eine gute Frau

PLURAL

M. F. N.

N.   **seine neuen Bücher**
G.   **seiner neuen Bücher**
D.   **seinen neuen Büchern**
A.   **seine neuen Bücher**

d. Adjectives that stand alone before a noun have the endings of the definite article in all cases except the genitive singular of the masculine and neuter, where they end in **-en**:

SINGULAR

	Masc.	*Neuter*	*Fem.*
N.	**guter Mann**	**gutes Kind**	**gute Frau**
G.	**guten Mannes**	**guten Kindes**	**guter Frau**
D.	**gutem Mann**	**gutem Kind**	**guter Frau**
A.	**guten Mann**	**gutes Kind**	**gute Frau**

PLURAL

M. F. N.

gute Eltern
guter Eltern
guten Eltern
gute Eltern

17. Nouns formed from the adjectives or participles follow the rules for the adjective declension:

der Alte	the old man	**ein Alter**	an old man
der Reisende	the traveler	**ein Reisender**	a traveler
der Gefangene	the prisoner	**ein Gefangener**	a prisoner

18. Adjectives following **viel,** *much,* **wenig,** *little,* **etwas,** *something,* **nichts,** *nothing,* are regarded as neuter nouns:

wenig Gutes   little good   **etwas Schönes**   something nice

19. Comparison of Adjectives

To form the comparative, add **-er** to the stem of the adjective. To form the superlative, add **-(e)st**:

schnell quick **schneller** quicker
(der, die, das) schnellste (the) quickest

20. Monosyllabic adjectives with **a, o,** or **u** usually have an umlaut in the comparative and superlative:

> **kurz** short **kürzer** shorter **kürzeste** shortest

21. The superlative of a predicate adjective often has the form **am -(e)sten**:

> **Der Tag ist lang.** The day is long.
> **Die Woche ist länger.** The week is longer.
> **Das Jahr ist am längsten.** The year is the longest.

22. Irregular Comparison:

gut	good	**besser**	better
groß	large	**größer**	larger
hoch	high	**höher**	higher
nah	near	**näher**	nearer
viel	much	**mehr**	more

beste	best	**(am besten)**
größte	largest	**(am größten)**
höchste	highest	**(am höchsten)**
nächste	nearest	**(am nächsten)**
meiste	most	**(am meisten)**

23. Comparison of Equality: **(eben)so . . . wie, (genau)so . . . wie,** *as . . . as:*

> **(eben)so leicht wie** as easy as
> **Komm so schnell wie möglich.** Come as soon as possible.

24. Comparison of Inequality: adjective with the comparative ending **-er** followed by **als,** *than:*

> **Papier ist leichter als Eisen.** Paper is lighter than iron.

25. Adverbs

The uninflected forms of adjectives serve as adverbs:

Das Mädchen ist schön.   The girl is beautiful.
Sie singt schön.   She sings beautifully.

26. The superlative of the adverb is formed by **am -(e)sten**:

Er spricht am lautesten von allen.   He speaks the
loudest of all.

27. The absolute superlative **aufs -(e)ste** denotes an extreme
degree without definite comparison:

Er begrüßte mich aufs freundlichste.   He greeted
me in the most friendly manner.

28. The adverb **gern** adds the element of liking; it has an
irregular comparison: **lieber, am liebsten**:

Ich trinke gern Milch.   I like to drink milk.
Er trinkt lieber Kaffee.   He prefers to drink coffee.
Sie trinkt am liebsten Tee.   She likes (to drink) tea
best.

29. Possessive Adjectives

mein	my	**unser**	our
dein	your (*fam. sing.*)	**euer**	your (*fam. pl.*)
sein	his	**ihr**	their
ihr	her	**Ihr**	your (*polite sing. and pl.*)
sein	its		

30. The possessive adjectives follow the declension of the
indefinite article (**ein, eine, ein**):

mein Freund   my friend
meine Frau   my wife
mein Kind   my child
Er hat Ihren Bleistift, Ihr Buch und Ihre Tasche.   He
has your pencil, your book, and your bag.

31. The Possessive Pronouns

The possessive pronouns are the same as the possessive
adjectives but follow the declension of the definite article:

Ist das sein Buch? — Nein, es ist ihres.   Is this his
book? — No, it is hers.
Das ist nicht ihr Garten sondern unserer.   This is
not their garden but ours.

32. Demonstrative Adjectives and Pronouns

SINGULAR				PLURAL	
Masc.	*Fem.*	*Neuter*		*All Genders*	
dieser	**diese**	**dieses**	this	**diese**	these
jener	**jene**	**jenes**	that	**jene**	those

33. Demonstrative adjectives and demonstrative pronouns
have the same forms. They follow the declension of the
definite articles:

**Dieser Tisch, diese Lampe und dieses Buch gehören
mir.**   This table, this lamp, and this book belong to me.
**Der Besitzer dieses Tisches, dieser Lampe und
dieses Buches ist nicht hier.**   The owner of this table,
this lamp, and this book is not here.
**Ich spreche von diesem Tisch, dieser Lampe, und
diesem Buch.**   I am talking about this table, this lamp,
and this book.
**Sie sehen diesen Tisch, diese Lampe und dieses
Buch.**   You see this table, this lamp, and this book.

34. The demonstrative pronouns **der, die, das** have no
equivalent in English. Especially in the nominative,
dative, and accusative cases they take the place of a
personal pronoun and usually stand at the beginning of
the sentence. They have the same forms as the relative
pronouns based on the definite article and refer to a
previously mentioned noun.

Gefällt dir die Musik? — Nein, die ist zu laut.   Do
you like the music? — No, it is too loud.
Das Hotel ist gut.   In dem möchte ich wohnen.   The
hotel is good. I'd like to stay in it.
Der Mann ist langweilig. Den will ich nie wieder

sehen. The man is dull. I don't want to see him again.

Das sind zwei schöne Bäume. Die sind schon 100 Jahre alt. These are two beautiful trees. They are already 100 years old.

Das ist Eva und das ist John. Die sind schon oft hier gewesen. This is Eva and that is John. They've often been here.

NOTE: **das** can refer to all nouns in the singular and plural.

35. Personal Pronouns

PERSON	NOMINATIVE		DATIVE		ACCUSATIVE		REFLEXIVE	
1	**ich**	I	**mir**	(to) me	**mich**	me	**mir** *or* **mich**	(me) myself
2	**du**	you (*fam.*)	**dir**	(to) you	**dich**	you	**dir** *or* **dich**	(you) yourself
3	**er**	he	**ihm**	(to) him	**ihn**	him	**sich**	himself
	sie	she	**ihr**	(to) her	**sie**	her	**sich**	herself
	es	it	**ihm**	(to) it	**es**	it	**sich**	itself
1	**wir**	we	**uns**	(to) us	**uns**	us	**uns**	ourselves
2	**ihr**	you (*fam.*)	**euch**	(to) you	**euch**	you	**euch**	yourselves
3	**sie**	they	**ihnen**	(to) them	**sie**	them	**sich**	themselves
	Sie	you (*polite sing. and pl.*)	**Ihnen**	(to) you	**Sie**	you	**sich**	yourself *or* yourselves

The genitive of the personal pronouns is rare.

36. Pronominal Compounds: **da-** and **wo-**

The dative and accusative of personal pronouns governed by prepositions are replaced by **da-** when they refer to inanimate objects:

> **Er schreibt mit der Feder; er schreibt damit.**   He writes with the pen; he writes with it.
>
> BUT:
>
> **Er geht mit seinem Freund; er geht mit ihm.**   He goes with his friend; he goes with him.

a. Pronominal compounds with **da-** can also anticipate a dependent clause:

> **Ich bin dafür, daß er kommt.**   I am for it that he should come.
> **Ich bin dagegen, früh aufzustehen.**   I am against getting up early.

b. If the preposition begins with a vowel, **dar-** must be used:

> **darin** in it   **darauf** on it   **darüber** about it

c. Similar compounds are formed with **wo-** when an inanimate object is referred to in questions:

> **Woran denkt er?**   What is he thinking of?
> BUT: **An wen denkt er?**   Whom is he thinking of?
>
> **Wovon reden Sie?**   What are you talking about?
> BUT: **Von wem reden Sie?**   Whom are you talking about?

37. Interrogative Pronouns and Adjectives

a.

	Masc. and Fem.		*Neuter*	
N.	**wer**	who	**was**	what
G.	**wessen**	whose	—	
D.	**wem**	to whom	—	
A.	**wen**	whom	**was**	what

b.

	SINGULAR			PLURAL	
	Masc.	*Fem.*	*Neuter*	*All Genders*	
N.	**welcher**	**welche**	**welches**	**welche**	which, what
D.	**welchem**	**welcher**	**welchem**	**welchen**	to which, what
A.	**welchen**	**welche**	**welches**	**welche**	which, what

The genitive is not used.

   c. **was für ein(e), was für**   what kind of (cf. 5)
      worum   about what
      womit   with what, etc. (cf. 36c)
      wieviel   how much
      wie viele   how many

      NOTE: **Der wievielte ist heute?**   What date is today?

38. Relative Pronouns

SINGULAR

	Masc.	*Fem.*	
N.	**der (welcher)**	**die (welche)**	who, which, that
G.	**dessen**	**deren**	whose
D.	**dem (welchem)**	**der (welcher)**	to whom, which
A.	**den (welchen)**	**die (welche)**	whom, which, that

	Neuter	
N.	**das (welches)**	who, which, that
G.	**dessen**	whose
D.	**dem (welchem)**	to whom, which
A.	**das (welches)**	whom, which, that

PLURAL

All Genders

N.	**die (welche)**
G.	**deren**
D.	**denen (welchen)**
A.	**die (welche)**

a. In all relative clauses the inflected verb stands last:

Ich kenne den Mann, der eben hier war.   I know the
man who was here just now.

**Die Frau, deren Hut auf dem Tisch liegt, ist meine
Schwägerin.**   The lady whose hat is lying on the table
is my sister-in-law.

b. If the antecedent is an indefinite neuter form, such as
alles, vieles, etwas, nichts, manches, or a neuter
adjective-noun in the superlative, **was** replaces **das
(welches):**

Alles, was Sie sehen, ist neu.   All that you see is new.

Das ist das Schönste, was ich je gesehen habe.   This
is the most beautiful (thing) that I have ever seen.

Was is also used to refer to the idea of a preceding
clause:

**Er sagte, er wolle nicht kommen, was mich sehr
ärgerte.**   He said he didn't want to come, which made
me very angry.

c. A relative pronoun must always be expressed; it cannot merely be implied:

The book you referred to is in the library. = **Das Buch,
das Sie erwähnten, ist in der Bibliothek.**

d. **Wer,** *whoever*, and **was,** *whatever*, are indefinite relatives without antecedents:

Wer nicht wagt, der nicht gewinnt.   Whoever does
not venture does not gain.   (Nothing ventured, nothing
gained.)

Was er sagt, verstehe ich nicht.   What(ever) he says,
I don't understand.

e. When the relative pronoun refers to an inanimate
object and is preceded by a preposition, it may be
replaced by the **wo-** construction:

Das Buch, wovon Sie sprechen, ist interessant.   The
book that you are speaking of is interesting.

39. Negatives

   a. **Nicht,** *not,* expresses negation with verbs, adverbs, and adjectives:

     Das geht nicht. That does not work (go).
     Das Auto fährt nicht schnell. The car does not go fast.
     Das Bild ist nicht schön. The picture is not beautiful.

   b. **Kein, keine,** *no* or *not a,* is used before nouns:

     Das weiß kein Mensch. No person knows that.
     Das dauert keine Stunde. That does not take an hour.

40. Word order

   a. In main clauses the inflected verb is always the second element, whatever the first element may be:

     Der Mann kommt immer erst spät abends nach Hause.
     Immer kommt der Mann erst spät abends nach Hause.
     Erst spät abends kommt der Mann immer nach Hause.
     Nach Hause kommt der Mann immer erst spät abends.
     The man never comes home until late at night.

   b. In questions *without* an interrogative particle, the verb stands first:

     Gehen Sie jetzt nach Hause? Are you going home now?
     Haben Sie das nicht gelesen? Didn't you read this?

   c. In questions *with* an interrogative particle, the verb comes second:

     Warum wollen Sie schon gehen? Why do you want to leave already?
     Wann kommt der Zug? When does the train arrive?

   d. Time expressions usually precede place expressions:

Ich bin am ersten Januar in Hamburg angekommen.
I arrived in Hamburg January first.

e. Position of objects. The direct object noun follows the indirect object (noun or pronoun); the direct object pronoun precedes the indirect object (noun or pronoun):

Er gab dem Mann das Geld.   He gave the money to the man.
Er gab ihm das Geld.   He gave him the money.
Er gab es ihm.   He gave it to him.
Er gab es dem Mann.   He gave it to the man.

f. The past participle and the infinitive are placed last in main clauses:

Ich habe schon sehr viel von Ihnen gehört.   I have already heard a great deal about you.
Ich werde Ihnen bald einen Brief schreiben.   I'll write you a letter soon.

Or they are placed first for emphasis:

Gesehen habe ich ihn noch nicht, aber gehört habe ich von ihm.   I haven't seen him yet, but I have heard of him.
Schreiben kann er nicht, aber lesen kann er ganz gut.   He cannot write but he can read quite well.

41. Dependent Word Order

In dependent clauses (introduced by subordinating conjunctions, interrogatives used indirectly, or relative pronouns), the inflected verb stands last:

Er kann nicht kommen, weil er keine Zeit hat.   He cannot come because he hasn't got time.
Ich weiß nicht, wann er kommen wird.   I don't know when he will come.
Das ist der Mann, der den Koffer gebracht hat.   This is the man who brought the trunk.

Note that all dependent clauses must be separated by a comma from the main clause.

42. Conjunctions

a. Coordinating: **und,** *and,* **aber,** *but, however,* **sondern,** *but,* **denn,** *for,* **oder,** *or,* **entweder . . . oder,** *either . . . or,* **weder . . . noch,** *neither . . . nor*

When coordinating conjunctions connect main clauses, they do not cause any change in word order:

Der Tisch ist gedeckt, und wir können sofort essen.
The table is set, and we can eat right away.
Entweder miete ich mir ein Zimmer, oder ich muß im Hotel bleiben.   Either I rent a room or I must stay in the hotel.
Er fährt nicht mit dem Zug, sondern er fliegt mit dem Flugzeug.   He is not going by train, but he is flying.

Note that **sondern** is used instead of **aber** after a negative statement that forms a contrast with the following clause.

Coordinating conjunctions may also be used to connect words and phrases:

Er kam, sah und siegte.   He came, saw, and conquered.
Er ist groß aber nicht schwer.   He is tall but not heavy.

Some coordinating conjunctions require inverted word order, with the verb coming second. Important examples: **außerdem,** *besides,* **dennoch,** *yet,* **nur,** *only,* **daher, deshalb,** *therefore,* **sonst,** *otherwise.*

Wir müssen uns beeilen, sonst kommen wir zu spät.   We must hurry, otherwise we'll be too late.
Er hat in England studiert ; daher spricht er so gut Englisch.   He studied in England; therefore he speaks such good English.

b. Subordinating: **als,** *when,* **als ob,** *as if,* **bis,** *until,* **damit,** *so that,* **daß,** *that,* **bevor,** *before,* **ehe,** *before,* **falls,** *in case,* **nachdem,** *after,* **ob,** *whether, if,* **obgleich, obwohl,** or **obschon,** *although,* **seit(dem),** *since,* **während,** *while,* **weil,** *because,* **wenn,** *if*

Subordinating conjunctions introduce dependent clauses:

Er wußte nicht, daß er im falschen Zug saß. He didn't know that he was sitting in the wrong train.

NOTE: When a subordinate clause precedes the main clause, it counts as the first element of the sentence and the verb of the main clause follows immediately:

Nachdem wir unsere Mahlzeit beendet hatten, rauchten wir eine Zigarre. After we had finished our meal we smoked a cigar.

43. als, wann, wenn

a. **als,** *when,* used as conjunction, refers to a past event:

Als wir auf die Straße gingen, sahen wir den alten Turm. When we walked down the street, we saw the old tower.

b. **wann,** *when,* is an interrogative:

Wann fahren Sie nach Deutschland? When are you going to Germany?
Ich weiß nicht, wann er abfährt. I don't know when he is leaving.

c. **wenn,** *if* or *when(ever)*:

Wenn er kann, kommt er. If he can, he'll come.
Immer wenn er kommt, bringt er etwas mit. Whenever he comes, he brings something along.

44. Tenses of the Verb (that differ from English)

a. The present indicative is often used to denote future:

Er fährt morgen nach Berlin.   Tomorrow he will be traveling to Berlin.

It is also used to indicate that an action started in the past and is continuing into the present. In such a case English uses the present perfect:

Wie lange sind Sie schon hier? How long have you been here?

Ich bin seit zwei Jahren in Deutschland.   I have been in Germany for two years.

NOTE: **schon,** *already,* and **seit,** *since,* are commonly used with the present tense with this meaning.

b. The imperfect indicative is used to indicate that an action was still continuing when another action started, whereas English uses the past perfect:

Ich ging schon eine halbe Stunde, als ich ihn sah.   I had been walking for half an hour when I saw him.

The imperfect denotes a customary act or condition:

Früher trank er viel.   He used to drink a lot.

Immer wenn ich ihn traf, grüßte er mich.   Whenever I met him, he would always greet me.

c. The future indicative may be used idiomatically to express conjecture or probability in the present:

Er wird wohl zu Hause sein.   He is probably at home.

Sie werden wohl verstehen, was ich meine.   You will probably understand what I mean.

d. The future perfect may be used similarly to express conjecture or probability in the past:

Er wird es wohl getan haben.   He probably did it.

Sie werden wohl schon davon gehört haben.   You probably heard about it already.

NOTE: The word **wohl** adds the element of probability.

e. The present perfect takes the place of the imperfect in isolated statements, questions, and in conversation:

Das habe ich mir gedacht.   I thought so.
Wann sind Sie gestern abend nach Hause gegangen?
When did you go home last night?
Ich bin heute morgen angekommen und habe mir gleich ein Zimmer gemietet.   I arrived this morning and rented a room right away.

45. Separable Prefixes

If a prefix of a verb has an independent meaning and it is stressed, it is usually separable:

kommen, to come, **ankommen,** to arrive, **aufkommen,** to come up, **herauskommen,** to come out, **wegkommen,** to get away, **vorbeikommen,** to come by

a. In main clauses prefixes separate from their verbs in the present, imperfect, and imperative:

Er steigt in den Zug ein.   He gets on the train.
Er stieg in den Zug ein.   He got on the train.
Steigen Sie in den Zug ein!   Get on the train!

b. In dependent clauses prefixes do not separate:

Ich sehe, daß er in den Zug einsteigt.   I see that he is getting on the train.

c. The separable prefix forms a compound with the regular past participle:

angekommen, arrived, **aufgemacht,** opened, **ausgegangen,** gone out

d. The prefix also forms a compound with a dependent infinitive preceded by **zu:**

Er hat keine Lust anzufangen.   He has no desire to start.

e. Separable prefixes are always stressed:

ab'fahren, to depart, **zu'gemacht,** closed, **ein'zutreten,** to enter

46. Inseparable Prefixes

Inseparable prefixes have no independent meaning and are never stressed: **be-, emp-, ent-, er-, ge-, ver-, zer-** :

> **verge'ben,** to forgive, **behal'ten,** to keep, **gefal'len,** to please

Er erholt sich gut.   He is recovering well.
Er erholte sich gut.   He recovered well.

In forming the past participle with an inseparable prefix the usual **ge-** is omitted:

> **brechen,** to break, **gebrochen,** broken
> **zerbrechen,** to break (to pieces), **zerbrochen,** broken

47. Reflexive Verbs

Reflexive verbs are very common in German.

a. The reflexive pronouns **mir/mich, dir/dich, sich, uns, euch** (cf. §34) are used frequently, as in English. They act as direct or indirect objects that refer action back to the subject:

Ich sehe mich im Spiegel.   I see myself in the mirror.
Er/sie wäscht sich.   He/she washes himself/herself.
Du mußt dir selbst helfen.   You must help yourself.
Sie gestatten sich selbst viele Freiheiten.   They permit themselves many liberties.

NOTE: The definite article and the reflexive pronoun in the dative are used when referring to parts of one's body or clothing:

Wasch dir die Hände.   Wash your hands.
Sie putzte sich die Zähne.   She was brushing her teeth.

Zieh dir die Jacke an! Put on your coat!
Ziehen Sie sich den Mantel aus! Take off your overcoat.

b. There are many reflexive verbs in German whose English equivalent is non-reflexive. They can be translated by an ordinary verb (**sich benehmen,** *to behave*), by a passive form (**sich ärgern über,** *to be annoyed at*), or by a verbal phrase (**sich freuen auf,** *to look forward to*).

Other examples:

sich interessieren für   to be interested in
sich fürchten vor   to be afraid of
sich wundern über   to be surprised at
sich irren   to be mistaken
sich erinnern an   to remember
sich etwas ansehen   to look at something

c. Reflexives may be used in the plural to imply reciprocity, sometimes emphasized by **gegenseitig,** *each other, one another:*

sich (gegenseitig) beschimpfen   to curse one another
Sie küßten sich.   They kissed (each other).

48. Impersonal verbs indicating:

a. Phenomena of nature:
Es donnert. It is thundering.
Es friert. It is freezing.

b. Physical or mental conditions:
Es freut mich/dich/ihn/sie/uns/euch/sie/Sie. I am glad/you are glad, etc.
Es tut mir/dir/ihm/ihr/ihm/uns/euch/ihnen/Ihnen leid. I am sorry/you are sorry, etc.

49. The Modal Verbs

können	to be able to	**sollen**	to be supposed to, to be obliged to
dürfen	to be allowed to		
mögen	to like to	**wollen**	to want to, to intend to
müssen	to have to		

a. The present indicative of modals:

ich kann/darf/mag/muß/soll/will (schreiben)
du kannst/darfst/magst/mußt/sollst/willst (schreiben)
er kann/darf/mag/muß/soll/will (schreiben)
wir können/dürfen/mögen/müssen/sollen/wollen (schreiben)
ihr könnt/dürft/mögt/müßt/sollt/wollt (schreiben)
sie ⎱
Sie ⎰ **können/dürfen/mögen/müssen/sollen/wollen (schreiben)**

b. The imperfect of modals is regularly weak, except for the loss of the umlaut in all forms and the change from **g** to **ch** in **mögen**:

ich konnte/durfte/mochte/mußte/sollte/wollte
wir konnten/durften/mochten/mußten/sollten/wollten

c. The past participles of modals have weak forms but without an umlaut and with **ch** for **mögen.** They are only used when the modal functions as a normal verb.

er hat gekonnt/gedurft/gemocht/gemußt/gesollt/gewollt
Er hat es gewollt.   He wanted it.

d. The infinitive is used as a past participle for all modals when there is a dependent infinitive. This construction is called the "double infinitive":

Ich habe gestern einen Brief schreiben können.   I was able (lit., have been able) to write a letter yesterday.

Er wird morgen kommen wollen.   He'll want to come tomorrow.

Er wird es wohl haben tun dürfen.   He probably was allowed to do it.

e. The preposition **zu** is omitted with infinitives that depend on modal verbs:

Er kann kommen.   He is able to (can) come.

Er mußte die Stadt verlassen.   He had to leave the city.

f. Other verbs that form the double infinitive and do not require **zu** with a dependent infinitive:

sehen	to see	**helfen**	to help
hören	to hear	**lassen**	to let, have (something done)
gehen	to go		
fahren	to go (by vehicle)	**lernen**	to learn

Er geht schwimmen.   He is going swimming.

Er lernt fliegen.   He is learning to fly.

NOTE: In combination with most other verbs the infinitive is used together with **zu.**

Er hat angefangen zu arbeiten.   He started to work.

g. The double infinitive is always the last element in a clause, even in a dependent clause:

Ich weiß, daß er es gestern abend hat machen wollen.
I know that he wanted (has been wanting) to do it last night.

NOTE: These constructions sound stilted in conversation and are usually replaced by the imperfect:

Ich weiß, daß er es gestern abend machen wollte.

50. The True Passive

a. The true passive voice is formed with the verb **werden** and the past participle (the agent is expressed by **von**):

Der Brief wird von dem Mann gelesen. The letter is read by the man.

Der Gast wurde vom Hausherrn empfangen. The guest was received by the host.

b. **worden** instead of **geworden** is used as the past participle of **werden** in passive compound tenses:

Der Koffer ist von dem Gepäckträger gebracht worden. The trunk was brought (has been brought) by the porter.

51. The true passive is often replaced by an active form.

    a. When the subject is not a person and may be expressed by the indefinite pronoun **man:**

Hier wird Deutsch gesprochen. German is spoken here.

OR: **Hier spricht man Deutsch.** (lit., One speaks German here.)

Es wurde gegessen und getrunken. There was eating and drinking.

OR: **Man aß und trank.** (lit., One ate and drank.)

    b. When a form of the verb **sein** followed by **zu** and an infinitive can replace a passive construction with a modal verb:

Er kann nicht gesehen werden. He cannot be seen.

OR: **Er ist nicht zu sehen.** (lit., He is not to be seen.)

    c. When the reflexive form of **lassen (sich lassen)** is used with an infinitive:

Das kann gemacht werden. That can be done.

OR: **Das läßt sich machen.** (That lets itself be done.)

52. The subjunctive is used in wishes and exhortations:

Wäre er doch hier! I wish he were here.

Wenn ich ihn nur sehen könnte! If I could only see him.

Ich möchte gern eine Reise machen.   I should like to take a trip.

And in softened statements and polite phrases:

Ich würde ihn gern sprechen.   I should like to speak to him.

Dürfte ich um das Salz bitten.   May I ask for the salt?

53. The subjunctive in conditional sentences denotes a condition contrary to fact:

Wenn er mein Freund wäre, würde ich es ihm sagen. If he were my friend (but he is not), I would tell him (lit., tell it to him).

Wenn wir früher aufgestanden wären, hätten wir mehr Zeit.   If we had risen earlier (but we didn't), we would have more time.

54. The subjunctive is used after **als ob,** *as if:*

Er tat, als ob er es nicht gehört hätte.   He acted as if he had not heard it.

55. The subjunctive in commands and directions:

Gehen wir jetzt!   Let us go now.

Man nehme zwei Eier und etwas Milch.   Take two eggs and some milk.

56. The subjunctive in indirect (reported) speech. In spoken language both the past and present subjunctive are used.

Der Mann sagte, er hätte (habe) es gesehen.   The man said that he had seen it.

Er fragte mich, ob ich kommen könnte (könne).   He asked me whether I could come.

Er sagte, ich sollte (solle) ihm helfen.   He said I should help him.   *Or:* He told me to help him.

NOTE: In conversation the subjunctive is usually replaced by the indicative in such indirect phrases, especially when the main verb is in the present:

Der Mann sagt, er hat es gewußt.   The man says that he has known it.

57. **wissen, kennen, können,** *to know*

  a. **wissen,** to know facts

   Ich weiß, wo er wohnt.   I know where he lives.

  b. **kennen,** to be acquainted with, know about

   Kennen Sie den Mann?   Do you know this man?

  c. **können,** to know how to do something (languages, physical activities, or skills)

   Können Sie Deutsch?   Do you know German?

   Er kann nicht Auto fahren.   He does not know how to drive a car.

  NOTE: cf. §49 for the modal function of **können.**

58. Common Features of Verbs

  a. All infinitives end in **-en** or **-n**:

   kommen   to come   **handeln**   to act

  b. The present indicative endings are the same for all verbs, with only a few exceptions:

ich	geh **e**	I go, am going
du	geh **st**	you (*fam. sing.*) go, are going
er		he
sie }	geh **t**	she } goes, is going
es		it
wir	geh **en**	we go, are going
ihr	geh **t**	you (*fam. pl.*) go, are going
sie	geh **en**	they go, are going
Sie	geh **en**	you (*polite, sing. and pl.*) go, are going

NOTE: Verbs whose infinitive stems end in **-d** or **-t** insert an **e** before consonant endings: **er arbeitet, bindet,** etc. Verbs whose infinitive stems end in **s** or **z** use contractions for the **du** form: **du heißt** instead of **heißest, du sitzt** instead of **sitzest.**

c. The future tense is formed with the present indicative of **werden** and the infinitive:

ich	**werde**	**gehen (schlafen, essen)**	I shall go (sleep, eat)
du	**wirst**	**gehen (schlafen, essen)**	you will go, etc.
er sie } es	**wird**	**gehen (schlafen, essen)**	
wir	**werden**	**gehen (schlafen, essen)**	
ihr	**werdet**	**gehen (schlafen, essen)**	
sie	**werden**	**gehen (schlafen, essen)**	
Sie	**werden**	**gehen (schlafen, essen)**	

d. All intransitive verbs that denote a change of place or of condition use the verb **sein** to form the compound past tenses:

Ich bin gekommen.   I have come.
Er ist gewachsen.   He has grown.

Likewise: **sein,** *to be,* and **bleiben,** *to remain*

Er ist hier gewesen.   He has been here.
Wir sind dort geblieben.   We have remained there.

All other verbs (transitive, reflexive, and those intransitive verbs that denote rest or state) use **haben** as an auxiliary:

Was haben Sie gemacht?   What did you do?
Ich habe mich gewaschen.   I have washed myself.
Wo hat er gestanden?   Where did he stand?
Haben Sie gut geschlafen?   Did you sleep well?

e. The future perfect is formed with the future tense of **sein,** respectively **haben,** together with the past participles:

Er wird gekommen sein.   He will have come.
Sie wird gearbeitet haben.   She will have worked.

f. The present participle is formed by adding **-d** to the infinitive:

tanzend   dancing   **schlafend**   sleeping
gehend   going

NOTE: As in English, the present participle is often used as an adjective, in which case it must then follow the rules for adjective declension:

der arbeitende Mann   the working man
ein arbeitender Mann   a working man

It is also used as adverb:

Er ging singend und pfeifend fort.   He went away singing and whistling.

59. Weak Verbs

Weak verbs are of the same type as English "regular" verbs:

tanzen	**er tanzte**	**er hat getanzt**
to dance	he danced	he has danced

a. Imperfect:

ich	tanz **te**	I was dancing	arbeit **ete**	I was working
du	tanz **test**	(danced, did	arbeit **etest**	(worked, did
er		dance, etc.)		work, etc.)
sie	tanz **te**		arbeit **ete**	
es				
wir	tanz **ten**		arbeit **eten**	
ihr	tanz **tet**		arbeit **etet**	
sie	tanz **ten**		arbeit **eten**	
Sie	tanz **ten**		arbeit **eten**	

NOTE: If the stem of a verb ends in **-d** or **-t,** the ending **-ete** is added. (See **arbeitete** above.)

b. The past participle is formed by adding **-(e)t** to the stem of the verb with the **ge-** prefix:

Er hat getanzt.   He has danced.
Er hat gearbeitet.   He has worked.

c. All regular weak verbs form the present indicative
   regularly (cf. §58b):

du mach**st**   you make
er leg**t**   he lays
du spiel**st**   you play

60. Strong Verbs

Strong verbs are of the same type as English "irregular"
verbs:

singen	**er sang**	**er hat gesungen**
to sing	he sang	he has sung

a. Imperfect:

ich	sang		I sang (was	fuhr		I traveled (was
du	sang	**st**	singing, did	fuhr	**st**	traveling, did
er	sang		sing, etc.)	fuhr		travel, etc.)
wir	sang	**en**		fuhr	**en**	
ihr	sang	**t**		fuhr	**t**	
sie	sang	**en**		fuhr	**en**	
Sie	sang	**en**		fuhr	**en**	

b. The past participle is formed by adding the ending
   -en to the changed verb stem with the **ge-** prefix:

singen	**gesungen**	**schreiben**	**geschrieben**
to sing	sung	to write	written

c. According to the vowel change (**ablaut**), strong verbs
   may be divided into seven groups:

   I. ei-ie-ie *or* ei-i-i: **bleiben**, to remain, **blieb, geblie-
      ben ; reiten,** to ride, **ritt, geritten**
   II. ie-o-o: **schießen,** to shoot, **schoß, geschossen**
   III. i-a-u: **trinken,** to drink, **trank, getrunken**
   IV. e-a-o: **gelten,** to be valid, **galt, gegolten**
   V. e-a-e: **geben,** to give, **gab, gegeben**
   VI. a-u-a: **fahren,** to drive (travel), **fuhr, gefahren**

VII. a, au, o, u, ei-ei — same vowel as infinitive:

halten, to hold, **hielt, gehalten**
laufen, to run, **lief, gelaufen**
stoßen, to push, **stieß, gestoßen**
heißen, to be called, **hieß, geheißen**

d. Irregular Present Indicative

Strong verbs with the stem vowel **e** form the 2nd and 3rd person singular of the present indicative irregularly:

sehen	to see	**nehmen**	to take	**geben**	to give
du siehst	you see	**nimmst**	you take	**gibst**	you give
er sieht	he sees	**nimmt**	he takes	**gibt**	he gives

Strong verbs with the stem vowel **a, au,** or **o** add umlaut (˜) to the 2nd and 3rd person singular of the present indicative:

schlagen	to beat	**laufen**	to run	**stoßen**	to push
du schlägst	you beat	**läufst**	you run	**stößt**	you push
er schlägt	he beats	**läuft**	he runs	**stößt**	he pushes

61. Irregular Verbs

a. **sein** (*to be*)

PRESENT		IMPERFECT	PAST PARTICIPLE
ich	bin	war	gewesen
du	bist	warst	
er	ist	war	
wir	sind	waren	
ihr	seid	wart	
sie	sind	waren	
Sie	sind	waren	

b. **haben** (*to have*)

ich	habe	hatte	gehabt
du	hast	hattest	
er	hat	hatte	

PRESENT	IMPERFECT	PAST PARTICIPLE
wir haben	hatten	
ihr habt	hattet	
sie haben	hatten	
Sie haben	hatten	

c. **werden** (*to become*)

ich werde	wurde	geworden
du wirst	wurdest	
er wird	wurde	
wir werden	wurden	
ihr werdet	wurdet	
sie werden	wurden	
Sie werden	wurden	

d. **wissen** (*to know*)

ich weiß	wußte	gewußt
du weißt	wußtest	
er weiß	wußte	
wir wissen	wußten	
ihr wißt	wußtet	
sie wissen	wußten	
Sie wissen	wußten	

e. **kennen** (*to know*)

(regular)		
	ich kannte	gekannt
	du kanntest	
	er kannte	
	wir kannten	
	ihr kanntet	
	sie kannten	
	Sie kannten	

NOTE: **brennen,** *to burn,* **rennen,** *to run,* **nennen,** *to name,* **senden,** *to send,* and **wenden,** *to turn,* are conjugated like **kennen.** (The imperfect of **senden** is **sandte,** of **wenden, wandte.**)

PRESENT	IMPERFECT	PAST PARTICIPLE

f. **bringen** (*to bring*)

    (regular)   ich brachte   gebracht

g. **denken** (*to think*)

    (regular)   ich dachte   gedacht

62. Indicative Mode

	WEAK		STRONG

Present:

ich kauf **e**	I buy (am	komme **e**	I come (am
du kauf **st**	buying,	komm **st**	coming,
er kauf **t**	do buy, etc.)	komm **t**	do come, etc.)
wir kauf **en**		komm **en**	
ihr kauf **t**		komm **t**	
sie kauf **en**		komm **en**	
Sie kauf **en**		komm **en**	

Imperfect:

ich kauf **te**	I bought (was	kam	I came (was
du kauf **test**	buying, did	kam **st**	coming, did
er kauf **te**	buy, etc.)	kam	come, etc.)
wir kauf **ten**		kam **en**	
ihr kauf **tet**		kam **t**	
sie kauf **ten**		kam **en**	
Sie kauf **ten**		kam **en**	

Present Perfect:

ich **habe** **gekauft** etc.	I have bought (*or* I bought)	ich **bin** **gekommen** etc.	I have come (I came)

Past Perfect:

ich **hatte** **gekauft** etc.	I had bought	ich **war** **gekommen** etc.	I had come

Future:

ich **werde**	I shall (will)	ich **werde**	I shall (will)
kaufen	buy	**kommen**	come
etc.		etc.	

Future Perfect:

ich **werde**	I shall have	ich **werde**	I shall have
gekauft	bought	**gekommen**	come
haben		**sein**	
etc.		etc.	

63. Subjunctive Mode

	WEAK	STRONG

Present Meaning:

ich kauf **te**	käm **e**
du kauf **test**	käm **est**
er kauf **te**	käm **e**
wir kauf **ten**	käm **en**
ihr kauf **tet**	käm **et**
sie kauf **ten**	käm **en**
Sie kauf **ten**	käm **en**

Past Meaning:

ich **hätte gekauft**	**wäre gekommen**
du **hättest gekauft**	**wärest gekommen**
er **hätte gekauft**	**wäre gekommen**
wir **hätten gekauft**	**wären gekommen**
ihr **hättet gekauft**	**wäret gekommen**
sie **hätten gekauft**	**wären gekommen**
Sie **hätten gekauft**	**wären gekommen**

Future Meaning:

ich **würde kaufen**	**würde kommen**
du **würdest kaufen**	**würdest kommen**
er **würde kaufen**	**würde kommen**
wir **würden kaufen**	**würden kommen**
ihr **würdet kaufen**	**würdet kommen**

| sie **würden kaufen** | **würden kommen** |
| Sie **würden kaufen** | **würden kommen** |

64. Forming the Past and Present Subjunctive

The subjunctive with present meaning is formed from the past indicative (hence it is called the "past subjunctive"):

  a. Weak verbs use the past indicative without any change:

    Wenn ich das kaufte, hätte ich kein Geld mehr. If I bought this, I would have no more money.

  b. Strong verbs use the stem of the imperfect indicative and add the endings **-e, -est, -e, -en, -et, -en** and an umlaut (¨) if the vowel is **a, o,** or **u**:

    Wenn er liefe, käme er schneller hin (würde er schneller hinkommen). If he ran, he would get there more quickly.

  c. The modals (**können, dürfen,** etc.) and the verbs conjugated like **kennen (rennen, nennen, brennen, senden, wenden)** form a regular weak imperfect for the past subjunctive:

    Wenn Sie es wollten, könnte ich Ihnen helfen. If you wished, I could help you.

  d. **bringen, denken, wissen** use the imperfect indicative with an umlaut: **brächte, dächte, wüßte.**

  e. **sein** counts as a strong verb: **wäre.**

  f. The present subjunctive (used practically only in indirect speech) is formed by adding the endings **-e, -est, -e, -en, -et, -en** to the infinitive stem of all verbs:

    er sag-e, kenn-e, komm-e. Only exception: **ich sei, er sei.**

65. Imperative Mode

    a. Regular:

Gehe! (Geh!)	Go!	(**du** is understood)
Geht!	Go!	(**ihr** is understood)
Gehen Sie!	Go!	(**Sie** must be expressed)

    b. Irregular:

All strong verbs with an irregular present indicative (**i** or **ie** forms) form the second person singular (**du** form) accordingly:

Sieh! See!   **Nimm!** Take!   **Gib!** Give!

    c. Indirect commands are formed from the present subjunctive:

Gehen wir!   Let's go.
OR: **Laßt uns gehen.** (more common)

Er gehe!   Let him go.
OR: **Laß ihn gehen.** (more common)

66. Principal Parts of Strong and Irregular Verbs

As a rule, only simple verbs and compound verbs with inseparable prefixes are shown. Compound verbs with separable prefixes are included only if they appear in the text but the main verb does not.

An asterisk (*) before the past participle indicates that the verb is conjugated with **sein** instead of **haben.**

INFINITIVE	PRESENT (3rd pers. sing.)	IMPERFECT (sing.)	PAST PARTICIPLE
anerkennen (to recognize)	erkennt . . . an	erkannte . . . an	anerkannt
anfangen (to begin)	fängt . . . an	fing . . . an	angefangen
beißen (to bite)	beißt	biß	gebissen
beginnen (to begin)	beginnt	begann	begonnen
bekommen (to get, receive)	bekommt	bekam	bekommen
besitzen (to possess)	besitzt	besaß	besessen
besprechen (to discuss)	bespricht	besprach	besprochen
bestehen (aus) (to consist of)	besteht	bestand	bestanden
biegen (to bend)	biegt	bog	gebogen
bieten (to offer)	bietet	bot	geboten
binden (to bind)	bindet	band	gebunden
bitten (to ask, request)	bittet	bat	gebeten
bleiben (to remain)	bleibt	blieb	* geblieben
braten (to fry)	brät	briet	gebraten
brechen (to break)	bricht	brach	gebrochen
brennen (to burn)	brennt	brannte	gebrannt
bringen (to bring)	bringt	brachte	gebracht
denken (to think)	denkt	dachte	gedacht
dürfen (to be allowed)	darf	durfte	gedurft
empfehlen (to recommend)	empfiehlt	empfahl	empfohlen
erfahren (to find out)	erfährt	erfuhr	erfahren
erraten (to guess)	errät	erriet	erraten

INFINITIVE	PRESENT (3rd pers. sing.)	IMPERFECT (sing.)	PAST PARTICIPLE
erscheinen (to seem, to appear)	erscheint	erschien	* erschienen
essen (to eat)	ißt	aß	gegessen
fahren (to ride, to go by)	fährt	fuhr	* gefahren
fallen (to fall)	fällt	fiel	* gefallen
fangen (to catch)	fängt	fing	gefangen
finden (to find)	findet	fand	gefunden
fliegen (to fly)	fliegt	flog	* geflogen
fließen (to flow)	fließt	floß	* geflossen
frieren (to freeze)	friert	fror	gefroren
geben (to give)	gibt	gab	gegeben
gefallen (to please)	gefällt	gefiel	gefallen
gehen (to go)	geht	ging	* gegangen
gelingen (to succeed)	gelingt	gelang	* gelungen
gelten (to be valid)	gilt	galt	gegolten
genießen (to enjoy)	genießt	genoß	genossen
geschehen (to happen)	geschieht	geschah	* geschehen
gestehen (to admit)	gesteht	gestand	gestanden
gewinnen (to win)	gewinnt	gewann	gewonnen
gießen (to pour)	gießt	goß	gegossen
haben (to have)	hat	hatte	gehabt
halten (to hold)	hält	hielt	gehalten
hängen (to hang) (also regular)	hängt	hing	gehangen

Infinitive	Present	Past	Past Participle
heißen (*to be called*)	heißt	hieß	geheißen
helfen (*to help*)	hilft	half	geholfen
hinterlassen (*to leave*)	hinterläßt	hinterließ	hinterlassen
kennen (*to know*)	kennt	kannte	gekannt
klingen (*to sound*)	klingt	klang	geklungen
kommen (*to come*)	kommt	kam	* gekommen
können (*to be able to*)	kann	konnte	gekonnt
laden (*to load*)	lädt	lud	geladen
lassen (*to let, to leave*)	läßt	ließ	gelassen
laufen (*to run*)	läuft	lief	* gelaufen
leihen (*to loan, borrow*)	leiht	lieh	geliehen
lesen (*to read*)	liest	las	gelesen
liegen (*to lie*)	liegt	lag	gelegen
mögen (*to like*)	mag	mochte	gemocht
müssen (*to have to*)	muß	mußte	gemußt
nehmen (*to take*)	nimmt	nahm	genommen
nennen (*to name*)	nennt	nannte	genannt
raten (*to advise*)	rät	riet	geraten
reiben (*to rub*)	reibt	rieb	gerieben
reißen (*to tear*)	reißt	riß	gerissen
rennen (*to run*)	rennt	rannte	* gerannt
rufen (*to call*)	ruft	rief	gerufen
scheinen (*to seem; to shine*)	scheint	schien	geschienen
schieben (*to push*)	schiebt	schob	geschoben

INFINITIVE	PRESENT (*3rd pers. sing.*)	IMPERFECT (*sing.*)	PAST PARTICIPLE
schlafen (*to sleep*)	schläft	schlief	geschlafen
schlagen (*to beat*)	schlägt	schlug	geschlagen
schließen (*to close*)	schließt	schloß	geschlossen
schmeißen (*to throw*)	schmeißt	schmiß	geschmissen
schneiden (*to cut*)	schneidet	schnitt	geschnitten
schreiben (*to write*)	schreibt	schrieb	geschrieben
schwimmen (*to swim*)	schwimmt	schwamm	* geschwommen
sehen (*to see*)	sieht	sah	gesehen
sein (*to be*)	ist	war	* gewesen
singen (*to sing*)	singt	sang	gesungen
sinken (*to sink*)	sinkt	sank	* gesunken
sitzen (*to sit*)	sitzt	saß	gesessen
sprechen (*to speak*)	spricht	sprach	gesprochen
springen (*to bounce*)	springt	sprang	* gesprungen
stehen (*to stand*)	steht	stand	gestanden
stehlen (*to steal*)	stiehlt	stahl	gestohlen
steigen (*to climb*)	steigt	stieg	* gestiegen
tragen (*to carry*)	trägt	trug	getragen
treffen (*to meet; to hit*)	trifft	traf	getroffen
treten (*to step*)	tritt	trat	* getreten
trinken (*to drink*)	trinkt	trank	getrunken
tun (*to do*)	tut	tat	getan

übertragen (*to transmit*)	überträgt	übertrug	übertragen
umgeben (*to surround*)	umgibt	umgab	umgeben
unterbrechen (*to interrupt*)	unterbricht	unterbrach	unterbrochen
unternehmen (*to undertake*)	unternimmt	unternahm	unternommen
verbieten (*to forbid*)	verbietet	verbot	verboten
verbinden (mit) (*to connect*)	verbindet	verband	verbunden
verbringen (*to spend*)	verbringt	verbrachte	verbracht
verderben (*to spoil*)	verdirbt	verdarb	verdorben
vergessen (*to forget*)	vergißt	vergaß	vergessen
verlassen (*to leave*)	verläßt	verließ	verlassen
verlieren (*to lose*)	verliert	verlor	verloren
verschreiben (*to prescribe*)	verschreibt	verschrieb	verschrieben
verstehen (*to understand*)	versteht	verstand	verstanden
verzeihen (*to forgive*)	verzeiht	verzieh	verziehen
wachsen (*to grow*)	wächst	wuchs	* gewachsen
waschen (*to wash*)	wäscht	wusch	gewaschen
wegstoßen (*to kick away*)	stößt . . . weg	stieß . . . weg	weggestoßen
werden (*to become*)	wird	wurde	* geworden
werfen (*to throw*)	wirft	warf	geworfen
wiegen (*to weigh*)	wiegt	wog	gewogen
wissen (*to know*)	weiß	wußte	gewußt
wollen (*to want, to wish*)	will	wollte	gewollt
zergehen (*to dissolve*)	zergeht	zerging	* zergangen
ziehen (*to pull*)	zieht	zog	gezogen

67. Countries and Places, Nationalities and their Derivative Adjectives

Amerika	Amerikaner/Amerikanerin	amerikanisch
Argentinien	Argentinier/Argentinierin	argentinisch
Berlin	Berliner/Berlinerin	berlinisch
Brasilien	Brasilianer/Brasilianerin	brasilianisch
Chile	Chilene/Chilenin	chilenisch
China	Chinese/Chinesin	chinesisch
Dänemark	Däne/Dänin	dänisch
Deutschland	Deutscher/Deutsche	deutsch
England	Engländer/Engländerin	englisch
Europa	Europäer/Europäerin	europäisch
Frankreich	Franzose/Französin	französisch
Griechenland (Greece)	Grieche/Griechin	griechisch
Hamburg	Hamburger/Hamburgerin	hamburgisch
Holland	Holländer/Holländerin	holländisch
Italien	Italiener/Italienerin	italienisch

Japan	Japaner/Japanisch	japanisch
Kanada	Kanadier/Kanadierin	kanadisch
Mexiko	Mexikaner/Mexikanerin	mexikanisch
München	Münchner/Münchnerin	münchnerisch
Norwegen (Norway)	Norweger/Norwegerin	norwegisch
Österreich (Austria)	Österreicher/Österreicherin	österreichisch
Polen (Poland)	Pole/Polin	polnisch
Portugal	Portugiese/Portugiesin	portugiesisch
Rußland (Russia)	Russe/Russin	russisch
Schweden	Schwede/Schwedin	schwedisch
die Schweiz (Switzerland)	Schweizer/Schweizerin	schweizerisch
Spanien	Spanier/Spanierin	spanisch
die Türkei	Türke/Türkin	türkisch
Venezuela	Venezolaner/Venezolanerin	venezolanisch

EXAMPLES: **Sie ist Französin.** She is French. **Der Wein ist spanisch.** The wine is Spanish. **Der englische Humor.** The English humor.

INDEX TO GRAMMAR
AND USAGE